The African Testament of GOD
African Sacred Text Project

Alateme Sonari

DEDICATION

To all who love FREEDOM, PEACE & SELF
DETERMINATION

CONTENTS

	Introduction	i
1	Chapter: The DIVINE & The Cultural Gods	1
2	Chapter: The DIVINE & The Christian God	4
3	Chapter: The Need for an African Testament of GOD	8
4	Chapter: Foreign Cultural Gods are not Your Gods	13
5	Chapter: Transformation of Consciousness	19
6	Chapter: Obstacles Along the Way	25
7	Chapter: The Family as the Sacred Temple	32
8	Chapter: Voice of our Ancestors	42
9	Chapter: African Spiritual Vision	56
10	Chapter: Personal Responsibility	67
11	Chapter: The Direct Line	76
12	Chapter: Famous Sacred Texts	79
13	Chapter: New World Spiritual Vision	104
14	Bibliography	124

INTRODUCTION

Thank you for checking out the African Sacred Text Project. I have thought about an African Sacred Text for a very long time. During the period I thought about the name of our sacred text. First a title flashed through my mind: The African Testament of GOD. But that seemed too long so I decided to use the first letters of each word in the title and came up with the acronym TATOG. Next I considered the prevailing creation stories in the world and thought that we could add more to the stories with our present knowledge of Past Life Regression and Quantum Physics. Then I thought about our experiences as a people in the world. In the United States for example the Slave Trade, the Plantation System, Segregation, Black Oppression, Black Inventors, Black Olympic Glories, Black Poets, Racial Discrimination and Prejudice came to mind. In Africa I thought about the Slave Trade, the Apartheid Regime, Colonization, African Freedom Fighters, African Independence and African Poets. In the Caribbean I thought about Afro-Caribbean freedom fighters, Afro-Caribbean music, Afro-Caribbean Olympic Glory and Afro-Caribbean poets.

I did not stop there and as my meditation continued I began to consider the contents of the TEXT including the books in it. The following books crossed my mind: the Book of Creation, the Book of Gods, the Book of Saviors, the Book of Teachers, the Book of Sacred Texts, the Book of Religions, the Book of Love, the Book of Life, the Book of Knowledge, the Book of Moral Laws, the Book of Psalms, the Book of Proverbs and the Book of the Family.

In the Book of Teachers the Buddha, Christ, Krishna, Confucius, Lao Tsu, Zoroaster, Guru Nanak, Mahavira, Mahatma Gandhi, Mother Theresa, Dr. King and President Nelson Mandela came to mind. In the Book of Saviors I thought about John Brown, Abraham Lincoln, Dr. King, Oprah Winfrey, the Dalai Lama, Mother Theresa, President Nelson Mandela, Mia Angelou, Malcolm X, Rosa Parks, Colin Powell, Booker T. Washington, William Wilberforce, Bessie Coleman, Paul Laurence Dunbar,

Henry Browne, Frederick Douglas, Harriett Tubman, Paul Robeson, Kwame Nkrumah of Ghana, Haile Selassie of Ethiopia, Kenneth Kaunda of Zambia, Julius Nyerere of Tanzania, Jomo Kenyatta of Kenya, Robert Mugabe of Zimbabwe, Patrice Lumumba of Congo, Nnamdi Azikiwe of Nigeria, Obafemi Awolowo of Nigeria, Abubakar Tafawa Balewa of Nigeria and the Afro-Caribbean Freedom Fighters.

I know the above list is not exhaustive but it is a place to start. I also know that not every African or member of the African Diaspora would welcome an African Sacred Text. Thus the main purpose of this book is to share the reasons why it is very important to have an African Sacred Text at this time. Number 1 on the list of those who might oppose an African sacred text would be some members of other religions and with good reasons. Number 2 on the list are African preachers who have a vast empire of supporters with assets in the millions. It is easy to reject what is good for everyone when you are the only one who is benefiting from the present system, but it takes guts and wisdom to walk away from millions in order to change the lives of millions of people.

I have often told my family to walk away from anything that benefits them but hurts another creature; we are counting on you! Number 3 on the list are Africans and members of the African Diaspora who have been brainwashed to believe that nothing good could come out of Africa. These people wholeheartedly believe that they are saved because they are members of foreign religions. They believe that they would go to heaven because of their affiliation. Little do they know that their membership to any religion created by humans has nothing to do with what the DIVINE has planned for them! This serves as a challenge for the rest of us to organize and make the African Testament of GOD a reality!

We are at a point in human history when it is our turn to significantly affect the world for the good of all creatures. We have an opportunity to set the stage to rid the world of religious exclusivity and extremism. There is no place in our world for any religion that promotes fundamentalism, extremism and exclusivity because **such actions are not of the DIVINE!** If you really want to know how GOD works you do not need to open any sacred text; just learn from the sun, the rain and the snow. When the sun shines there is no requirement to meet in order to enjoy it. When the rain falls it waters all our crops without conditions, and when the snow falls it invites all to play. In all these cases there is no membership, there are no membership fees and there are no tithes! **You can say the same thing about going to heaven; everyone goes to heaven because it is our reward for living on this planet**.

Have you noticed that in almost all the near death experiences no one comes back and says categorically that he or she saw a cultural God? In most cases they see their family members. Why? They see their family members because they are the people who really love them! Think about it. The purpose of the religion of membership is to elevate cultural Gods for earthly benefit and separate you from the unconditional Love of the DIVINE! It is now your call to put an end to the religion of membership and elevate the Almighty GOD!

The Almighty GOD treats all of us with unconditional love. There are no chosen people and we do not need to accept GOD because GOD is within us. Humans created the religion of acceptance in order to boost membership but how can you accept what you already have? The Almighty GOD has given each of us freedom to live our lives according to our experiences and not the experiences of others and definitely not from foreign sacred texts! The experiences of foreigners are not your experiences or the experiences of your people irrespective of how they embellish them. The Almighty GOD has blessed all creatures without conditions and loves you without requirements so there is no need to accept a foreign God. Anything contrary to this is an attempt to control, dehumanize and enslave others.

The second purpose of this book is to serve as an invitation card to all Africans and members of the African Diaspora for their support for the African Sacred Text Project. We need writers, donors, web site builder, IT consultants, accountants, attorneys and educators. If you are a writer I encourage you to first think of this project, sleep over it and take as much time as you can. At the end of your meditation, if you feel called to contribute to the African Testament of GOD I encourage you to prepare for the first meeting of the African Sacred Text project.

We also need donors for the Project. Some of the things we need include rental space for our meetings; Business Registration including Non-Profit Application; a Website; Publishing; Distribution; Offices in all African countries and everywhere there are members of the African Diaspora. We also need funds for travels to educate our people and our other brothers and sisters who may be interested in the African Sacred Text Project.

Attorneys, educators, accountants and all others who want to attend the first meeting of the African Sacred Text Project are encouraged to prepare for the event. What is at stake here is the general good—the good of a race of people and the good of the world. Do you see employment opportunities? Do you see free education for the poor up to college and beyond? Do you see more success, achievement and prosperity? Do you see an end to religious conflicts? Do you see the glorification of the Almighty GOD? Do you see wicked cultural Gods dethroned? Do you see our triumph over fear of hell? Do you see the shackles on our minds removed? Do you see our confidence soaring high? Do you see unity among religions? Do you see the possibilities? Write the African Testament of GOD!

The world does not become good when you are forced to worship a cultural foreign God! The world does not breathe when you are enslaved! The world does not rest when the contributions of your people are suppressed! The world stands still when there is discrimination, oppression and prejudice. Writing the African Testament of GOD is about FREEDOM; it is about EQUALITY; it is about TRUTH; it is about PEACE and it is about UNLIMITED OPPORTUNITIES! Write the African Testament of GOD; you can never be number one if you worship foreign cultural Gods because foreign cultural Gods only love their own people but the DIVINE loves you without conditions!

There is no doubt that some of you believe in foreign cultural Gods and foreign sacred texts with all your heart and I know what it means to have faith in GOD. But if your belief is based on what foreign texts tell you about what it means to be alive I encourage you to step back and re-examine your beliefs because the only thing worth believing in life are your own experiences and the experiences of your people. The experiences of others must never be the basis for your life. If it did that was a life that was never lived! Focus on your experiences and the experiences of your people and learn from them. The knowledge from your experiences is not something you read from books; it is the real stuff! Write the African Testament of GOD and motivate others who are in similar situations to write their own sacred texts. It is only when all our real historical stories are told that the world will experience peace!

There are many joys in life: the surge of creativity; the gift of a new born baby; the excitement of winning; the happiness of success; the peace of meditation; the companionship of marriage; the love of a mother, the equanimity of the developed mind, the opportunities of education and the bliss of cosmic consciousness but none of these is equal to the FREEDOM of a people who were once enslaved, dehumanized, lynched, marginalized, colonized and oppressed! It is your turn to be KING!

THE DIVINE & THE CULTURAL GODS

Throughout human history, people have sought to understand and name the sacred reality behind existence. In this search, two distinct categories emerge: the **DIVINE or the SOURCE** and the **Cultural Gods**.

The **DIVINE** refers to ultimate reality, the ineffable source of being, the transcendent and immanent ground that underlies and sustains all existence. It is beyond culture, time, and human definition. The Divine is infinite, eternal, and unbounded, often described as mystery, spirit, or the ultimate ground.

By contrast, **cultural gods** are particular deities shaped by the historical, social, and spiritual needs of a given people. They may embody nature, fertility, war, wisdom, or protection. These gods often bear human attributes, stories, and personalities, reflecting the imagination, fears, and aspirations of their worshippers.

Universality vs. Particularity
The Divine is universal. It transcends cultural and religious boundaries, appearing in different traditions as Brahman, the Dao, the One, the Ground of Being or Ultimate Mystery. The Divine is not owned by any tribe, race, or civilization; it is the source of life for all creation. Cultural Gods, on the other hand are particular. They belong to specific peoples and embody their historical context. For example, Zeus was the supreme God of the Greeks, Odin of the Norse, and Shango of the Yoruba. Each functions within a localized worldview and rarely claims universality beyond it. However historically the God of Christianity, Allah of Islam and Yahweh of Judaism are all cultural Gods irrespective of their present universal appeal.

Transcendence vs. Anthropomorphism
The **Divine** is beyond human categories. It is often described as

ineffable, formless, and beyond name. Philosophers and mystics insist that human language cannot capture the fullness of the Divine. Cultural Gods, by contrast, are anthropomorphic. They are given human shapes, voices, families, and emotions. They love and hate, wage war and reconcile, bless and curse. In many mythologies, Gods marry, fight, and even die. This human likeness makes them relatable but also limits their scope. Where the Divine is mystery beyond imagination, cultural Gods are mirrors of human life projected onto the heavens.

Absoluteness vs. Relativity

The **Divine** is absolute, the unconditioned ground of being. It does not depend on worshippers for existence. Even if no one acknowledged it, the Divine would still be. Cultural gods are relative. They gain power and identity from the devotion of their followers. When a people vanish or their culture shifts, their Gods often fade into myth. Once-vibrant deities like Baal, Isis, or Quetzalcoatl now survive largely as cultural memory rather than living realities of worship. Thus, the Divine stands as eternal presence, while cultural Gods rise and fall with human history.

Unity vs. Multiplicity

The **Divine** is often conceived in terms of unity. Even in traditions with many Gods, there is usually an acknowledgment of a supreme reality behind them. In Hinduism for example, Brahman is beyond the Gods and Devas; in Taoism, IT is the Tao and in African Mythology there is usually an unseen High God that is beyond and above all the cultural Gods. Mystics across cultures testify to this oneness as the heart of spiritual experience. Cultural Gods, however, are multiple by nature. They represent fragmented aspects of life: a God of the sea, a Goddess of fertility, a God of war, a God of Learning, a God of Creation or a God of the Harvest. Their multiplicity reflects the diversity of human concerns. In this way, the Divine represents the whole, while cultural Gods represent the parts.

Ultimate Source vs. Functional Role

The Divine is the ultimate source of existence itself. It is the reason there is something rather than nothing, the eternal ground upon which all life depends. Its role is not merely to intervene in human affairs but to be the infinite wellspring of reality. Cultural Gods, on the other hand, play functional roles. They are protectors, healers, warriors, or guides. They may govern natural forces or social order, but they do not usually claim to be the ultimate reality itself. Instead, they operate within the cosmos as powerful beings, not as its eternal ground. Where the Divine is the source of all, cultural Gods are agents within creation.

Conclusion

The distinction between the **Divine** and the **cultural Gods** is fundamental. The Divine is universal, transcendent, absolute, unified, and the ultimate source of being. Cultural Gods are particular, anthropomorphic, relative, multiple, and functional within human life. Yet, these categories are not opposed. Cultural Gods often serve as mediators through which people approach the Divine. They embody cultural memory, symbolizing aspects of the infinite in forms that communities can understand. In this sense, the Divine and the cultural Gods are not rivals but layers of humanity's attempt to encounter the sacred. Understanding their differences allows us to honor both: the Divine as the eternal mystery beyond all names, and the cultural Gods as the diverse expressions of human longing for the transcendent.

THE DIVINE & THE CHRISTIAN GOD

The words *"God"* and *"the Divine"* are often used interchangeably, yet they carry distinct meanings depending on their theological, philosophical, and cultural contexts. In Christianity, "God" refers specifically to the personal, revealed deity of the Bible, understood through the doctrines of creation, covenant, incarnation, and salvation. By contrast, the term *"the Divine"* is more expansive, encompassing the universal, transcendent, and immanent aspects of ultimate reality as conceived across different religious and philosophical traditions.

Personality vs. Abstraction

The Christian God is understood as a personal being who acts, speaks, loves, judges, and saves. He is the Creator of heaven and earth, revealed as Father, Son, and Holy Spirit in Trinitarian theology. In the Christian worldview, God is not merely a force or principle but an active, self-conscious reality who enters into relationship with humanity.

By contrast, **the DIVINE** is often described in more abstract terms. In philosophical discourse, it may be identified with the *Absolute*, the *Ground of Being*, or the *Infinite*. In some spiritual traditions, the Divine is not person-like at all, but rather the sacred quality present in existence ; energy, life-force, or cosmic order. For example, in Hindu thought, *Brahman* is beyond personal categories, while in Taoism, the *Tao* is the impersonal way that underlies reality. Thus, whereas the Christian God is emphatically *personal*, the Divine can be conceived as *impersonal* or even *non-theistic*.

Revelation vs. Intuition

The Christian God is known through revelation: God speaks through prophets, scriptures, and supremely through the incarnation of Jesus Christ. Christian faith emphasizes God's

4

initiative in the sense that humanity does not discover God by its own power but receives him as he reveals himself. Revelation is therefore specific, historical, and particular. **On the other hand,** the **DIVINE** is often encountered through *intuition, mystical experience, or philosophical reflection*. It is apprehended through the depths of consciousness, the awe of nature, or the silence of meditation. In this sense, the Divine is not bound to a single tradition but is accessible wherever human beings seek ultimate meaning. The Christian God on the other hand is culture bound! This is one of the reasons it is preached throughout the world to introduce him to people of other cultures. The DIVINE on the other hand cannot be taken to anywhere because IT is everywhere!

Exclusivity vs. Universality

Christianity traditionally teaches that the **Christian God** is the one true God, and that salvation comes uniquely through Jesus Christ. This gives Christianity an *exclusive* dimension: while acknowledging other Gods or Spirits, Christian theology often regards them as false, partial, or subordinate. In contrast, **the DIVINE** is often defined in universal terms. It may be seen as the common essence behind all religions, the shared sacred reality that different traditions interpret in diverse ways. Some Theologians and philosophers have argued that the DIVINE is a category broad enough to encompass Yahweh, Allah, Brahman, the Tao, and other manifestations of ultimate reality. However there are great differences between Yahweh, Allah and the Christian God on one side and the Tao and Brahman on the other side. Allah, Yahweh and the Christian God have a history and they tend to be culture bound while Brahman and the Tao tend to be universal because they are everywhere! Surely while the Christian God is identified with specific narrative, the DIVINE is inclusive and transcends cultural and doctrinal boundaries.

Relationship vs. Transcendence

The **Christian God** is relational: He loves, forgives, makes covenant, and calls humanity to fellowship. This relationship is grounded in the Trinity as Father, Son, and Spirit existing in eternal communion, and human beings are invited into that communion. Christian spirituality is therefore dialogical, based on prayer, worship, and relationship with a personal God. By contrast, **the DIVINE** is often emphasized in ITS transcendence. IT is the mystery beyond comprehension, the sacred presence that cannot be named or grasped. While the Divine may also be Immanent (within nature, within the self), it is often described as ineffable — beyond language and beyond relationship in the ordinary sense. Where Christianity emphasizes intimacy with God, many conceptions of the DIVINE emphasize reverence for mystery.

Salvation vs. Harmony

In Christianity, the **Christian God** offers *salvation* from sin, reconciliation with God, and eternal life. In this respect the human is seen as fallen but could be restored through Christ's sacrifice and resurrection. This makes the Christian God both a Creator and a Redeemer. The **DIVINE**, however, is often connected with *harmony* rather than salvation. Many traditions that speak of the DIVINE do not frame the human problem as "sin" but as ignorance, imbalance, or disconnection. The goal is not salvation through an external savior but awakening to oneness, balance with the cosmos, or alignment with the sacred order of life.

Conclusion

While the Christian God and the broader concept of the DIVINE share the notion of an ultimate, sacred reality, they differ significantly in personality, relationship with humanity, and philosophical underpinnings. The Christian God is a personal, relational cultural deity with a defined theological framework, whereas the DIVINE often refers to an impersonal, universal principle or consciousness accessible through mystical insight or philosophical reasoning. Understanding these distinctions enriches our grasp of religious diversity and the multifaceted nature of spirituality across cultures and traditions. It is thus clear that the Christian God is not universal but cultural. Cultural Gods belong to the cultures that raised them and have no place in other cultures!

Politics in Religion

When you worship a foreign God like Jesus or Allah as an African it means that you have no experiences or you've never lived or you have no regard for your Gods or you have no concept of what it means to be alive or you are foolish. When you use a foreign sacred text like the Bible or the Qur'an exclusively it also means your people have no experiences, they are foolish, they are not living, they are ignorant or they do not know what it means to be alive. Christianity and Islam are the worst things that happened to Africa and it is time to wake up from your hypnosis. Write the African Testament of GOD and be free!

THE NEED FOR AN AFRICAN
TESTAMENT OF GOD

Why must there be an African Testament of GOD? Because
Africa's wounds cry out for healing, and healing requires
testimony. For centuries, the Bible and the Qur'an were brought to
Africa not as gifts alone, but as instruments of subjugation. The
Word was twisted into chains, and faith became a weapon of
empire.

In this distortion, Africans were taught to see themselves not as
bearers of God's image but as cursed, inferior, and voiceless. Their
ancestral wisdom was dismissed as superstition, their prophets
silenced, their songs of praise forgotten.

But the DIVINE cannot be confined by colonizer's chains. Just as
slavery, apartheid and colonization ended, so Africa must rise to
reclaim the DIVINE inheritance stolen from her. The African
Testament of God is therefore not an invention, but a recovery. It is
Africa remembering what she always knew: that the DIVINE
walks with her, speaks through her, and calls her to testify to the
world.

This Testament is not for Africa alone. Just as the Upanishads and
the Tao Te Ching opened our eyes, so will Africa rise to heal and
bring hope to all nations. A new voice must be heard, lest the choir
of humanity remain incomplete.

Throughout history, religious texts and doctrines have served as
foundational guides for moral conduct, spiritual understanding, and
social cohesion. Prominent among these are the Bible, Quran,
Torah, the Bhagavad Gita, the Tao Te Ching, the Upanishads and

other sacred scriptures, each reflecting the cultural, historical, and spiritual landscapes of their respective communities. However, as Africa is a continent rich in diverse cultures, languages, and spiritual beliefs, there is a compelling need for an African Testament of GOD— a sacred document that embodies Africa's unique spiritual heritage, values, and understanding of the DIVINE.

The Cultural and Spiritual Diversity of Africa
Africa is home to thousands of ethnic groups, each with distinct traditions, languages, and spiritual practices. From the indigenous beliefs of the Yoruba, Ibo, Hausa, Ijaw, Zulu, and Maasai to the influence of Christianity, Islam, and traditional African religions, the continent's spiritual landscape is incredibly diverse. Existing religious texts often reflect the worldview of external civilizations or dominant religions, which may not fully encapsulate the indigenous philosophies and spiritual insights of African peoples.

Limitations of Foreign Religious Texts
While foreign sacred texts may have provided moral guidance and community cohesion, they often fall short in representing Africa's unique worldview. There are many limitations of foreign sacred texts and they include:

Cultural Disconnect: Most of these texts originate from different historical, geographical, and cultural contexts. Their narratives, metaphors, and moral teachings may not resonate with African realities.

Marginalization of Indigenous Beliefs: Traditional African religions have often been dismissed or misunderstood by outsiders, leading to their marginalization. This undermines the spiritual sovereignty of African communities.

Limited Ethical Frameworks for Contemporary Challenges:

Foreign Sacred Texts may lack specific guidance on issues such as environmental stewardship, communal rights, and social justice—areas deeply intertwined with indigenous African values.

Language and Accessibility Barriers: Translation issues and language barriers can hinder comprehension and engagement among local populations, especially in rural areas.

Rationale for an African Testament of GOD
Africa is a continent of profound spiritual depth, rich oral traditions, and diverse cosmological systems. Yet, the dominant sacred texts shaping African religious life—such as the Bible and the Qur'an—originate outside the continent. While these texts may have offered moral guidance and spiritual inspiration, they often reflect cultural assumptions, historical contexts, and theological frameworks that are foreign to African realities.

The African Testament of GOD is a call to spiritual sovereignty. It is a proposal to articulate the African understanding of the DIVINE, CREATION, MORALITY, and DESTINY in a sacred text authored by Africans for Africans. The rationale for such a text are many and we will draw from historical, philosophical, theological, and cultural perspectives.

Historical Context: Colonialism did not merely conquer land—it conquered minds and spirits. Missionaries often arrived alongside colonizers, presenting Christianity or Islam as superior to indigenous beliefs. African spiritual systems were dismissed as pagan, primitive, or demonic. Sacred groves were desecrated, ancestral rituals banned, and traditional healers persecuted.

This religious displacement created a spiritual vacuum. Africans were taught to seek GOD in foreign texts, foreign languages, and foreign rituals. The African Testament of GOD seeks to reverse this displacement by affirming that GOD has always spoken through African tongues, landscapes, and traditions.

Philosophical Foundations: African philosophy emphasizes relationships, communal ethics, and spiritual continuity. Concepts such as *Ubuntu* ("I am because we are"), *Ori* (personal destiny in Yoruba thought), and *Sankofa* (returning to retrieve what was lost) reflect a worldview where the DIVINE is immanent, ancestral, and communal.

Unlike Western dualism, African cosmologies often blur the boundaries between the sacred and the secular, the living and the dead, the human and the DIVINE. The African Testament of GOD would reflect this holistic ontology, offering a sacred narrative that aligns with African ways of knowing and being.

Theological Rationale: GOD is not absent from African traditions. The Supreme Being is known by many names including but not limited to Olodumare, Nyame, Chukwu, Ruhanga, Modimo or Tamuno and is often described as omnipotent, omnipresent, and benevolent. African spirituality includes rich hierarchies of divine beings, ancestors, and nature spirits. However, these theological insights remain scattered across oral traditions, rituals, and ethnographic records. The African Testament of GOD would consolidate and elevate these insights into a coherent sacred text, affirming that African theology is not folklore—it is DIVINE revelation.

Cultural Imperative: Narratives shape identity. When Africans rely solely on foreign scriptures, they risk internalizing foreign values, metaphors, and moral frameworks. The African Testament of GOD is a cultural imperative—a way to reclaim narrative sovereignty and affirm that African stories are sacred. This testament would draw from proverbs, myths, songs, rituals, and oral histories. It would honor the Griot as prophet, the elder as theologian, and the drum as scripture. It would be written in African languages, rhythms, and metaphors, making the DIVINE accessible and familiar.

Ethical Vision: African ethics emphasize balance, reciprocity, and communal responsibility. Taboos protect the sacred. Justice restores harmony. Elders guide the young. Proverbs encode moral wisdom. The African Testament of GOD would present these ethical principles as DIVINE commandments. It would offer a moral vision rooted in African values—one that affirms dignity, interdependence, and spiritual accountability.

African Diaspora: The African Diaspora mostly from slavery, migration, and exile carry fragments of African spirituality. In the Americas, Caribbean, and Europe, descendants of Africa have preserved spiritual practices through music, dance, and resistance. The African Testament of GOD would offer a spiritual homecoming. It would reconnect the Diaspora to ancestral wisdom, affirm their DIVINE heritage, and invite them to contribute their own sacred stories.

Communal Project: Unlike traditional scriptures written by elite scribes, the African Testament of GOD would be a communal project. Villages, families, and spiritual communities would contribute chapters, myths, prayers, and teachings. This decentralized methodology reflects African oral traditions and democratic spirituality. It affirms that revelation is not monopolized—it is shared.

A Living Testament: The African Testament of GOD is not a static book—it is a living testament. It evolves with each generation, each ritual, each revelation. It is not a rejection of other faiths—it is a reclamation of African divinity. By writing our own testament, we affirm that GOD has always spoken through Africa. We do not need permission to be sacred. We are the authors of our own spiritual destiny. Africa can never be free with a foreign spiritual vision! It is time to break the shackles on our minds and write the African Testament of GOD

FOREIGN CULTURAL GODS ARE NOT YOUR GODS

Humanity's religious imagination has always revolved around two layers of the sacred: the **DIVINE**, which is ultimate, transcendent, and universal, and the **Cultural Gods**, which are localized, particular, and reflective of community life. The distinction between these two realities is essential for understanding how human beings relate to the sacred.

The **DIVINE** is the source of all existence, often described as infinite, eternal, and ineffable. It is beyond human grasp, yet immanent in creation. It represents the unconditioned ground of being or the Ultimate Ground. "No tongue has touched IT", Joseph Campbell once said.

In contrast, **Cultural Gods** are specific manifestations of the sacred shaped by human culture, geography, and history. They embody natural forces, social functions, and human values in symbolic, personified form. These Gods vary across traditions and rise and fall with the people who venerate them.

Hinduism, Christianity, Taoism, Confucianism, Shinto, Islam, Janism, Sikhism and Buddhism are all foreign religions. The Bhagavad Gita, the Qur'an, the Tanakh, the New Testament, the Upanishads, the Dhammapada, the Tao Te Ching and the Avesta are all foreign sacred texts. Lord Shiva, Lord Brahma, Lord Vishnu, Lord Jesus, Lord Allah, Lord Buddha, Lord Yahweh and the Christian God are all foreign Gods.

Notice the difference between the cultural Gods and the DIVINE. The cultural Gods are tribal creations or manifestations. They are unique to the tribes or cultures that produced them; they are not the DIVINE. However tribal Gods could claim to be the DIVINE in a cultural, tribal or national context. For instance, in the Bhagavad Gita Lord Krishna gave Arjuna spiritual eyes in order to see the

Lord as the DIVINE. Arjuna's response when he saw the Lord as GOD is one of the most breath taking reactions in spiritual literature. In the New Testament the Lord Jesus also considers himself as GOD. In a basic Buddhist Mandala, there are 4 Buddhas, one at each corner of the Mandala. The central Buddha represents Ultimate Reality or GOD. In the Tanakh, Lord Yahweh also appeared to Moses as GOD. You can see that the idea of cultural Gods claiming to be the GOD of the Universe cuts across cultures but the truth is that none of them is the DIVINE!

What is the DIVINE or GOD?

The tribal Gods may take the form of GOD but none of them is the DIVINE because the DIVINE has no form. However if we consider the DIVINE as having a form then it must be many forms and not just one. But some cultures parade their Gods as the DIVINE. This is probably acceptable if the religions understand the multiplicity of forms. In other words if you believe that your God is the GOD of the Universe I expect you to know that I also believe that my God is the GOD of the Universe. If both of us agree on this premise there will be no need for me to force my God on you or for you to force your God on me. We can even worship the DIVINE together but in order to do so you must leave your image of GOD as well as your sacred text behind since both are the tribal or cultural elements that separate us. Here are some passages for further clarification:

I am the father of this universe, and even the source of the Father. I am the Mother of this universe, and the Creator of all. I am the Highest to be known, the path of purification, the holy OM, the three Vedas. Bhagavad Gita 9:17

For God so loved the world, that he gave his only begotten Son, that whosoever believeth in him should not perish, but have everlasting life. New Testament: John 3:16

I am the Way, and the Master who watches in silence; thy friend and thy shelter and thy abode of peace. I am the beginning and the middle and the end of all things: their seed of Eternity, their

Treasure supreme. Bhagavad Gita 9:18

Thomas said to him, "Lord, we don't know where you are going, so how can we know the way?" Jesus answered, "I am the way and the truth and the life. No one comes to the Father except through me. New Testament: John 14:5-6

If you cannot feel Me within it is not I. If someone has to convince you of My existence, it is not I. I AM the only Mystery that does not need an introduction. The Universal Holy Book

Masters of life may worship in foreign religious temples because they know and understand but the rest of us are stock with our images of GOD. The story of Shadrach, Meshach and Abednego is a classic case of being faithful to a cultural God in the midst of many Gods. Tanakh: Daniel 3:1-30

Once upon a time, Nebuchadnezzar ruled Babylon. He made a golden image and set it up for worship. At the sound of a drum everyone was required to fall down and worship the golden image. Anyone who did not worship the image would be thrown into a blazing fiery furnace. At the first sound of the drum everyone worshipped the golden image as directed by the king apart from Shadrach, Meshach and Abednego; Jews who served as officers in a province of Babylon. When the news concerning the three Jews came to Nebuchadnezzar he ordered to see them. The king asked them if it was true that they did not worship the Gods of Babylon and that they would not bow to the golden image at the sound of the drum? Shadrach, Meshach and Abednego confirmed the Kings suspicion but added that they worshipped a different God and would never worship his Gods or bow down to the golden image. So the king ordered his functionaries to put the three Jews into the fiery furnace.

According to the story the furnace was so hot that the soldiers who took the three men to the furnace were immediately burnt to death but the three Jews plus a fourth person were walking around in the furnace. When the king saw that Shadrach, Meshach and Abednego were not harmed in the furnace he asked them to walk out of the furnace. They inspected the three Jews to make sure that they were not harmed and truly they were all well. Thus King Nebuchadnezzar hailed the God of Shadrach, Meshach and Abednego and even promoted them and decreed that anyone who said anything against the God of the Jews would be killed.

In the same way we may refuse to bow down to any of the foreign Gods more especially Gods that were forced upon us. We are free and like Shadrach, Meshach and Abednego, we are not swayed by threats of damnation and we are not excited by promises of heaven. We have conquered all pairs of opposites in the world. The DIVINE within us is way more than any God out there and one who has the DIVINE has everything! Further, we cannot bow to the God of Shadrach, Meshach and Abednego because he is not our God. Most cultures have their cultural Gods and those are the only Gods that could save you because cultural Gods protect their people! Your belief in a foreign cultural Gods does not count because cultural Gods know that you could easily change your mind at any time. Further, if you believe in a foreign cultural God you stand the risk of being killed if your people are in a war with his people because cultural Gods only protect their people-not foreigners who believe!

Sonari's Differences Between the DIVINE and the Gods
1. GOD pervades the Universe; the Gods are local.
2. GOD is within all creatures; the Gods are invited.
3. GOD is unknowable; the Gods are known.
4. GOD is nameless; the Gods have names.
5. GOD is one; the Gods are many.
6. GOD loves all creatures without conditions; the Gods love you with conditions.
7. GOD has no chosen people; the Gods have chosen people.
8. GOD has no sacred place; the Gods have sacred places.
9. GOD unites all creatures; the Gods divide creatures.

10. GOD has no Sacred Text; the Gods have Sacred Texts.

11. GOD is neutral in human conflicts; the Gods take sides in human conflicts.

12. GOD does not judge us; the Gods judge us.

13. GOD takes us to heaven at the end; the Gods take us to hell at the end.

14. GOD is self-existing; the Gods exist because of you.

15. GOD is all-powerful; the Gods derive their power from you.

16. GOD exists in all cultures; the Gods can only be traced to specific cultures.

17. GOD is the Universal Spirit; the Gods are culture bound.

18. GOD does not accept sacrifices: the Gods accept sacrifices.

19. GOD leads us to Enlightenment; the Gods crave for our worship and adoration.

20. GOD will be waiting for us at the end; the Gods will not be there!

The Case against Allah

You may notice that I included Allah as one of the cultural Gods at the beginning of the chapter instead of as the GOD of the Universe. On the surface it appears that Moslems worship the DIVINE because Allah translates into GOD and I believe that the devotees think that they are worshipping GOD. There was actually a story on the Internet about a young man deciding to choose among the religions and he narrowed it down to Islam. According to his reasons, it is only Islam that has no images; all the other religions have images. This is not completely true because the Qur'an is regarded as the word of GOD in Islam and is therefore an image. **GOD has no sacred texts, hence Allah is also considered as one of the cultural Gods. Sorry!**

How is the African Testament of GOD Different?

Admittedly the African Testament of GOD is also a Sacred Text but it is not the word of GOD. Instead it is the collective historical experiences of mostly the African people and members of the African Diaspora written in spiritual language. You may call it "the works of GOD or the Spiritual Experiences of Africans. We can document the works of GOD in human experiences like the end of slavery; the end of colonization; the beginning of independence; the end of apartheid; the end of segregation; black Olympic glories; the contributions of African leaders to world peace and much more. The word of GOD on the other hand is spread throughout the Universe; the word of GOD is subject to individual interpretation but most important is that no text can contain it!

Spiritual Teachers in all Cultures

GOD did not send only one person to teach the whole world but has sent many spiritual teachers to all corners of the earth. Consider a situation in which foreign spiritual teachers are sent by GOD to save your people. Can you even conceive such a scenario? The Almighty GOD in all his wisdom and dominion is not able to produce spiritual teachers among you and has to resort to borrowing teachers from other cultures!

The idea is inconsistent with UNIVERSAL LOVE and serves to degrade the receiving culture. Surely this is not of GOD but of humans who want to dominate and to enslave others! Learn from history and examine every foreign idea thoroughly before incorporating it into your culture. Foreigners who are guilty of slavery, colonization, apartheid, racism and all the evils in society cannot and can never be the bearers of DIVINE message.

However, if there is any good in a foreign idea it must always remain subordinate to your own ideas. Your spiritual teachers are already amongst you and you do not need foreign spiritual teachers to save you. In short you do not need anyone to save you because the DIVINE has given you everything you need to save yourself from the world! The DIVINE is within you!

TRANSFORMATION OF CONSCIOUSNESS

When the world was at war during the Second World War, the United States played a significant role in ending the war and bringing freedom to the rest of the world. The major cause of the Second World War was the appetite for dominance and control by Hitler and his allies. In our time we can see the same thoughts in some religions. When a religion wants world dominance the thought is not different from that of Hitler and his allies. The fruits of dominance and control are fundamentalism, exclusivism, extremism and terrorism. Statements like "Every Knee Shall Bow" if not taken out of context and not misinterpreted run counter to our freedom and self determination.

Further "Every Knee Shall Bow" is more of an authoritarian demand than a DIVINE proclamation. The DIVINE has given us everything we need in this life but the cunning and greedy humans are using the DIVINE for profit and power. All power belong to the DIVINE and no human being, sacred text or God is qualified to tell you about the DIVINE because the DIVINE did not appoint pastors, evangelists, Imams and other spiritual leaders. You are a spiritual leader in your own right because the DIVINE resides within you!

Like the United States that made a difference in the Second World War you are called upon to put an end to religious dominance and control. GOD created your family to be in control of your spiritual life; not organized religions! A religion that tiers your family apart cannot be from GOD. Wake up from your hypnosis and see the organized religions for what they are! They are the real instruments of darkness and if you love your family you will have nothing to do with organized religions. One way of cutting ties with foreign organized religions is writing the African Testament of GOD! Here are some more reasons why it is absolutely necessary to write the African Testament of GOD:

World Peace

The African Testament of GOD is for world peace and the freedom of all people. It is written mostly to encourage Africans, members of the African Diaspora and the rest of the world to love their experiences and learn from others. Currently most religions have problems with competing religions; they preach against each other and sometimes they even kill each other. The African Testament of GOD will encourage all people to work together because it does not contain separatist or exclusive statements. Instead it calls all people to work together for the good of the world! In this respect fundamentalism, exclusivism, extremism and terrorism will give way to brotherhood and religion will no longer be at the center of our conflicts because in the end only our experiences matter and not the preaching of pastors nor the writings in foreign sacred texts.

Understanding
If you checked the top 30 poorest countries in the world you will find that most of them come from Africa. Corruption, drought, tribal wars and mismanagement may play some roles but an attitude of "GOD will provide" without doing anything could is the major factor. **The African Testament of GOD will highlight the fact that we are all already loved without conditions and blessed without requirements.** When people understand this TRUTH they'll have the motivation to change their lives with what they already have instead of waiting for a savior to descend from the heavens to change their lives. Admittedly many people who have issues or problems wish for the problems to disappear from their lives. The writers of the Bible knew this human tendency and used to as a recruitment strategy: "Join us and God will take away your problems and make you rich". Unfortunately this has never happened in this world and no one will descend from the heavens and make your life easier. If there is anyone in the whole world and out of the world who can help your life is YOU! So stop believing in the scam and start believing in yourself because the DIVINE is within you! Further no foreign God will save you; you have been deceived!

Education
Education is still a luxury in many African countries and as a result

many children roam the streets to earn a living. The last time I visited Nigeria, I was surprised at the number of children on the streets when they should be in schools. We hope to change this by giving free education to the poor. Education will also mean emphasizing African history and African religions in our schools as opposed to foreign history and foreign religions. According to the African Library Project:

- More than 1 in 3 adults cannot read.
- 182 million adults are unable to read and write.
- 48 million youths (ages 15-24) are illiterate.
- 22% of primary aged children are not in school.
- That makes 30 million primary aged children who are not in school.

My estimate is even more but even if there is only one illiterate child that is still unacceptable! I challenge African leaders who claim to love their people to give free primary, secondary and college education to their citizens. Education is the future of your progress but if you forego education in favor of foreign religions there is no way for Africa can rise. **If Africa must rise again it must invest heavily on education and expel all foreign religions in the continent including Christianity and Islam.**

Freedom

The Pope's or any other foreign religious leader's visit to an African country often brings an image of control and dominance to my view. I see Africans following quietly behind the foreign official in their own land and I am asking, "What are these people doing?" Has any African ever gone to a foreign land and taken control? Think seriously about this image and it will occur to you that we follow these foreign religious leaders because it is their religion and we worship their Gods. As long as you believe in foreign religions you will always be a slave! Become a leader in your land by writing the African Testament of GOD. So my brothers and sisters I know that spirituality is not about leadership but we can only be free when we worship our Gods instead of foreign Gods. Now think about this: GOD in all GOD'S WISDOM blessed only one nation with a sacred text and commanded other nations to follow this one nation because they are the chosen ones. How would you feel? For me that is a God that must never be allowed to enter our gates because such a God is promoting slavery, discrimination, terrorism, racism, extremism, fundamentalism and all that calls a nation to be ruthless.

Fortunately we do not have such a nation in the world because we have several sacred texts. We have hundreds if not thousands of sacred texts. It just happens that some of the sacred texts are more famous than others. Now the question is why do we have many sacred texts? The answer is simple: we have many sacred texts because we see GOD differently. Some see GOD through their tribal Gods and others see GOD through their sacred texts. Still others see GOD through their experiences. If we see GOD differently why should another culture force their version of GOD on us? Why should you worship a foreign God? Is it because you want to go to heaven or you do not want to go to hell?

As I said earlier "heaven" is your reward for living on this planet and no one can take it away from you. Thus if you worship a foreign God because of heaven or hell you can as well stop believing because the foreign Gods are not in charge! Forget about what is written in their sacred texts because the sacred texts tell different stories about heaven and hell. The question is which one do you choose? And the answer is none! The truth is that GOD has appeared to all people and fortunately Africans have all the experiences in real history to show the mighty hand of GOD in their lives. The Almighty GOD is calling upon us to share these experiences with the rest of the world. Our experiences on slavery, discrimination, colonization, apartheid, racism and oppression have no equals. These are the experiences the world wants to learn from you and they can be written in the African Testament of GOD!

I also encourage other cultures who want to write their own sacred texts to do the same. There is no glory or reward on earth or in heaven for believing in foreign sacred texts irrespective of what the texts promise. If the text does not teach about your experiences and the experiences of your people it is simply not your text! It is their text and their text can never be your text because your people did not write it. Like the Africans and members of the African Diaspora I encourage you to write your sacred texts and be FREE!

One last thought is the teaching that the Almighty GOD comes from a foreign culture, nation or race of people. If the Almighty GOD comes from another culture what does that say of your culture, race or nation? Not good enough, second class citizens, slaves, sinners or what? The truth is that GOD did not choose any culture. It is the humans who claim to be chosen by GOD to feel superior and to dominate other cultures. The result of dominance was slavery, colonization, apartheid, segregation, oppression, racism and the demise of African Gods. The unsuspecting natives easily believed the unscrupulous foreigners because they usually went with their sacred texts to prove that GOD was indeed on their side. It never occurred to the natives that the Almighty GOD would never do such things to any of his creation. Further they convinced you that your Gods were lesser Gods and their Gods were the real Gods and you believed them. In the process you abandoned your Gods and worshiped foreign Gods up to this day. From all indications a greater percentage of Africans and members of the African Diaspora worship foreign Gods. However now that you know the truth you can turn this around and put an end to the worship of foreign Gods! You are now in a position to break that mentality and open the door wide to the rest of the world. **GOD loves all creatures without conditions and blessed all creatures without requirements**! The foreign Gods only love their people and for the record the Almighty GOD did not come from a particular culture instead the Almighty GOD is within us and pervades the whole Universe.

Self-Determination
Foreign Gods are not your Gods and foreign sacred texts do not tell your stories. As long as you worship foreign Gods your experiences will ever remain in the background. Why would you spend eternity with a God that you do not even know? Why would you spend eternity with a God that has a chosen people? Many Africans have been sharing this same message for ages but you won't listen because of "handouts". As long as your appetite for

foreign handouts remains strong it may be difficult to break the shackles on your mind. History teaches us that those who have ever accomplished anything worthwhile learned from their own experiences and not from the experiences of others. Today the Almighty GOD is calling on you to remove your crutches, refuse all foreign handouts and take personal responsibility for the development of your mind and your life. Write the African Testament of GOD!

Right Thing to Do

Consider a situation in which the Arabs did not write their sacred text, the Qur'an. Would they become Jews or Christians? Would they have contributed anything to the world? What would have happened to them? The answers to these questions will be speculative but today we know that they ruled empires, influenced cultures and changed lives with the help of their religion. **The Kama Sutra teaches us that "the mortal gets what he wants" and in that vein there is no power in the world, above the world or beneath the world that could prevent you from writing the African Testament of GOD!**

Are you not ashamed of opening foreign sacred texts and reading about the contributions of their people? Who reads about the contributions of your people? Are you not hesitant about sponsoring foreign sacred texts? Who laughs to the bank when you buy foreign sacred texts? Could you use the proceeds from your sacred text for the development of your people? Who gets all the glory when you worship foreign Gods? Wake up Africa and take what is truly yours and change the course of world history. Write the African Testament of GOD and let the Almighty GOD use you to bring peace to the world! Write the African Testament of GOD and reap uncountable blessings and prosperity. It is your turn to be KING!

OBSTACLES ALONG THE WAY

I know that I am writing this book from a different level of consciousness. When I look back at my life I see how our levels of consciousness could take us prisoners in a world of possibilities. But with education coupled with our experiences we could rise above the limitations of our environment. Many Africans and members of the African Diaspora have thought about an African sacred text simply from the fact that most races in the world have their own sacred texts. Thus this idea has been with us for a long time and this book serves to motivate us to come together and make an African Testament of GOD a reality!

Like most of you I was raised in a religious family. My religion was a foreign religion. But at the crossroads of life I fired my foreign cultural God. That was one of the lowest points in my life but it was also the greatest thing I did for myself. It was the lowest point in my life because I was empty and hopeless. It was the greatest thing I did for myself because I found peace of mind after the event! While I was in that state of hopelessness and emptiness I thought about reading other sacred texts and I read among other texts the Upanishads, the Tao Te Ching, the Dhammapada and the Bhagavad Gita. My recovery was instantaneous. After reading the Upanishads I realized that I really didn't lose anything by firing my foreign God. I gained way more than I lost. I gained the DIVINE! The comparison between a tribal foreign God and the DIVINE is like day and night. For the first time in my life the scales fell from my eyes and I could see the DIVINE plainly-no sacred texts, no chosen people and no mediators! In a nutshell this is the most profound experience any human being could ever have!

But this realization has to be tested for it to become part of my life. I had a pastor that served as my spiritual adviser when I was in graduate school. The last time I saw him was when I needed someone to help me with my religious issues. I never saw him again after that until 3 years later. One day I stopped by the Computer Renaissance Store in Corvallis, Oregon and there he was. He told me he had left his former Church for another Church and invited me to attend his new church the next Sunday. I honored his invitation. This experience is significant because it was the first test of my state of mind after my breakthrough. My friend was already there when I arrived and people where coming in from all directions. This church is solely based on the Bible and as a result it was very popular in the community. Meanwhile he introduced me to some prominent members of the congregation and finally to the pastor. The first question the pastor asked me when we got introduced was "Are you saved?" I looked directly into his eyes with a smile and gladly responded in the affirmative and it felt good. I was finally psychologically free from my foreign cultural God!

The irony of this experience is that I was feeling good in a church in which accepting Jesus as your personal savior was the requirement for salvation. What has happened here? My only explanation is that the DIVINE transcends all categories and recognizing GOD within you opens the door to the Universe. In this sense one feels at home within the Universe and it doesn't matter whether you believe in Krishna, Jesus, Buddha or Confucius and it also doesn't matter if you do not believe at all! **What matters is that you have identified with the WHOLE rather than with any of the parts.** Thus until you identify with the WHOLE (DIVINE) all your religion is basically an empty endeavor!

Doomsayers

A greater percentage of the doomsayers would come from foreign cultural religions with their hands all over Africa. I am aware that some of these religions go to Africa to help and I commend you for your selfless services and I regard you as one of us in spite of your religion.

The remaining doomsayers will come from African preachers more especially the million dollar preachers. However I do not believe that all African million dollar preachers will counter our efforts for our own sacred text. Some of them really care for Africa and some are already doing a lot to help their fellow Africans. For all these people I say welcome aboard!

Beyond the doomsayers are our African Brothers and Sisters who want to know the best way to live their lives to achieve success and happiness. In most cases they don't know where they are going and they depend on others to show the way. I know that you have heard every promise from preachers and politicians and nothing materialized while you continue to suffer. This time I encourage you to believe in our project and believe in the Almighty GOD. As long as you believe in the Almighty GOD their messages of doom will not happen because your GOD is greater than their foreign Gods!

Now what will be their likely messages of doom? They could say that if you support the writing of the African Testament of GOD their God would end the world. But remember they have been saying this since I was 7 years old. I still remember the occasion when they told us that the world was going to end. I was doing some chores for my mother and when the message came I couldn't help but cry. My life was just beginning and a preacher was telling me that I was going to die? If you've lived as long as I have lived you have probably survived many "end of the world" scams but none of them came to pass. They did not come to pass because no one knows the manner in which human beings would be wiped out of the earth if such a thing will happen at all. **There are speculations but none of it will involve a metaphysical intervention from a cultural God.**

Assuming there is going to be a metaphysical intervention how could a cultural God say from India go and wipe out the Chinese? China is not his domain even if the Indian God claims to be the God of the Universe. If that happens there would be a war of the Gods because by nature cultural Gods protect their own people and the Chinese Gods would do everything in their power to protect their people. But there is not going to be a war of the Gods because no cultural God will descend from the heavens to kill non-believers or to judge the world for that matter! It is against UNIVERSAL LAW! Thus it is your right to believe or not to believe and no one, including the cultural Gods can take that away from you! I think the "end of the world" scam is a plot by some religious people to enrich themselves because people give and sometimes they give all their savings when they are told that the world would end in their life time. Do not be a victim to this religious scam! If you have faith in GOD, let it be an unadulterated faith! Faith based on sacred texts and religions are adulterated and they can never save you!

Next they might suggest that their foreign God would send all Africans who support the writing of the African Testament of GOD to hell. As I said earlier if their God is foreign, his domain is not in Africa and by UNIVERSAL LAW the foreign God cannot harm any African, let alone send them to hell. Further some might encourage you to distance yourself from anything that has to do with the writing of the African Testament of GOD for their foreign God to bless you. This is also another religious scam. GOD's blessing is not dependent on your actions. **Instead the Almighty GOD loves you without conditions and blesses you without requirements**. According to religious history cultural Gods are only loyal to their people and that is why they take the side of their people in wars against others. If you are worshipping a foreign God you must know that if your people have a war with the people of the foreign God the foreign God will take the side of his people and your faith will not even count. Thus if a preacher tells you that his foreign God will bless you, don't count on it. Besides, you don't need it because you already have the blessings of the Almighty GOD!

Finally some foreigners might sow seeds of discord among you. If they do not succeed in swaying you from supporting the African Testament of GOD they might try inciting one group against another. For instance they could sow seeds of discord between African nations, African Peoples or between Africans and members of the African Diaspora. Do not fall for any of these attempts to discourage your vision and remain united no matter what! Believe in your African Gods and believe in the Almighty GOD!

Skeptics

Skepticism is healthy and we want all skeptics on board to help us to produce a practical sacred text to help humanity. That being said what could be doubtful about writing the African Testament of GOD? Some might think that we do not have the resources for such a project. **This is not true because if you work with the Almighty GOD you don't need resources. All you need is a dream or a vision and GOD will provide the resources as you progress.** We already have the vision! Others may think that we do not have the spiritual backing for the project. This is also not true because our suffering cannot be compared to the sufferings of all the other peoples in the world put together. This may sound like an exaggeration but naming our sufferings could put them into perspective. Whose slave labor built the wealth of many nations? Whose land was occupied by foreigners with no regard for the owners of the land? Who were treated as second class citizens in their own land? Who were colonized? Who were lynched? Who were dehumanized? Who were really enslaved in human world history? You get the picture but we are not complaining because what is done is done; we just want to move forward! For the record, if other races have written their sacred texts no one can stop us from writing our own sacred text! There is no doubt that all African Gods are on our side but the GOD of the Universe is asking when you would share your experiences with the rest of the world? GOD lives through your experiences and it is time to let GOD SHINE!

Wet Blankets

The status quo seems comfortable because generally people do not like change. The average person for instance wants most things to remain the same for as long as they live. The truth is that everything changes on earth and the things that seem comfortable in our time were initiated by a few people who were not satisfied with the status quo. In the same way we can also change the things that work against us. If you are an African, not having your sacred text is not in your best interest. Until you advance your own spiritual vision of the world you will ever remain slaves to foreign Gods and their people. Thus if you think that writing the African Testament of GOD is too much trouble take a step back and consider the alternative. **The slavery of the mind is the last shackle on the African and only you can break it and let lose. Write the African Testament of GOD!**

Wolves in Sheep's Clothing

There are many well meaning people from other cultures who have helped Africans and continue to do so up to this day. However beware of the rich man who does not want the poor man to be rich like him and continues to give him handouts in order to keep him in his state of poverty. What you need are not handouts but the secret of the rich man's wealth and that secret is writing your own Sacred Text. Thus you must watch out for the foreigner who pretends to love you in order to discourage your vision. He will trick and frighten you and even predict the end of the world because of your vision. Do not listen to him irrespective of his promises of heaven and threats of hell because he is using a religious scam. If hell is real to you and you think you might go to hell when you pass on simply seek the protection of African Gods or the Almighty GOD and you will be saved! Remember African Gods are on your side whether you believe in them or not and they will never send their own to hell!

Take a Stand!

For how long will you continue to depend on foreigners for your spiritual well-being? For how long will you continue to be in foreign religious captivity? For how long will you continue to depend on foreign ideas on what it means to be alive? For how long will you continue to worship foreign Gods? For how long will you continue to believe in foreign religions? For how long will you continue to remain slaves to foreign Gods and their people? The foreigner will never approve of your Gods and as long as you worship his Gods you are still slaves!

When foreigners force their religious values on you they are in effect telling you that you have no worthwhile values. When foreigners force their religious books on you they are in effect telling you that you have no valuable experiences. When foreigners preach the works of their people in your lands they are in effect telling you that the experiences of your people do not count. When foreigners insist on the supremacy of their religions they are in effect telling you that your religions are inferior. When foreigners parade their religions in your lands they are in effect telling you that they still own you. When foreigners replace your Gods with their Gods they are in effect telling you that your Gods are unimportant and that you are better of being without a history and in continuous servitude.

THE FAMILY AS THE SACRED TEMPLE

In African traditional religions, spirituality is not confined to shrines, churches, or mosques. It is lived and embodied in the rhythms of daily life. Central to this worldview is the **family**, which functions not only as a social unit but also as a **sacred temple**, a place where the Divine, the ancestors, and the living converge in an unbroken chain of being. The family is the sacred nucleus of society, a microcosm of the cosmos, and a living sanctuary where rituals, values, and spiritual power are transmitted across generations. It is time to bring back the family as the main center for Africa's spiritual progress.

A Spiritual Bridge

African cosmologies generally view reality as consisting of two interconnected realms: the visible world of the living and the invisible world of ancestors, spirits, and the Divine. The family is the primary bridge between these realms and they include:

- **Ancestors** who remain part of the family and are honored through prayer, libations, and rituals. They continue to guide and protect the living.
- **The unborn** are also spiritually present, as fertility, birth, and continuity ensure that family lines endure.
- **The Divine** is accessed through the family unit, which becomes the sacred channel of life itself.

A Ritual Home

African societies maintain shrines, sacred groves, and communal altars, but the family home is the first temple. By situating rituals in the home, African societies emphasize that the sacred is inseparable from daily living. Many vital rituals begin and end in the family home and they include:

- **Naming ceremonies** to dedicate children to the community and ancestors.

- **Marriage rites** unite to families and affirm the sacredness of lineage.
- **Funeral rituals** to transform the home into a sacred temple for guiding the deceased into the ancestral world.
- **Libations** to sanctify family life, turning ordinary spaces into sacred ground.
- **Life Cycle Ceremonies** to celebrate a person's progression from one stage of life to the other like from an infant to an adolescent, from an adolescent to a teenager, from a teenager to an adult and from an adult to a senior citizen.

Home for Moral and Spiritual Values

In the absence of written scriptures, African societies transmit their wisdom and spirituality primarily through oral tradition. The family is the sacred school of values. This custodial role makes the family the guardian of both social order and spiritual heritage.

- **Elders** act as priests, judges, and teachers, preserving the spiritual memory of the community.
- **Parents** embody the moral authority of the ancestors and pass down virtues such as respect, truthfulness, generosity, and hospitality.
- **Proverbs, songs, and stories** are the sacred texts of the family temple, teaching children how to live harmoniously with others and with the cosmos.

Representative of Society & the Universe

African thought sees life as interconnected. The family is both a microcosm of society and a reflection of the universe itself. Consequently the family temple mirrors the structure of the wider cosmos, teaching individuals how to live harmoniously within creation.

- **Hierarchy mirrors cosmic order**: Elders represent authority, echoing the role of ancestors and deities.
- **Gender Roles** reflect cosmic dualities of male/female, earth/sky, sun/moon.

- **Children symbolize continuity**, embodying the principle of rebirth and the perpetuity of life.

The Family as Sacred Trust
African societies view the family as a divine trust, not merely a human construct. To nurture, protect, and extend the family is a spiritual duty. The family, therefore, is a sacred responsibility, and its breakdown is often seen not only as a social crisis but also as a spiritual disorder.

- Honoring parents and elders ensures blessings and continuity.
- Preserving lineage safeguards the living memory of the ancestors.
- Raising children well ensures that the family remains a strong spiritual temple into the future.

In African religions, the family is the first and most enduring temple of the sacred. It is where the Divine meets humanity, where ancestors remain alive, where rituals sanctify daily life, and where moral and spiritual values are preserved.

While shrines and community rituals hold their importance, the family remains the **foundation of African spirituality**, for it carries the living memory of the people, binds the visible and invisible worlds, and embodies the sacred trust of life itself.

To honor the family, therefore, is to honor the Divine. To preserve the family is to preserve the temple of God on earth. Writing the African Testament is another way of preserving the African way of life and African Spirituality for future generations.

The Sacred Space
Campbell once told his students at Sarah Lawrence College in New York that if they really want to help this world what they would teach is how to live in it. Now the question is: "How can we live in this world in order to be happy? It is definitely not about getting drunk or smoking some hallucinogenic drug or acquiring all the

materials the world has to offer. The next question is: How can we live in this world to be at peace? We cannot be at peace until we have peace within us. The final question is how can we live in this world to realize our dreams? The DIVINE is the Ultimate Giver; it gives rain to water our crops, the sun to maintain our lives, and the snow that invites us to play. In the same way the DIVINE also gives you the desires of your heart but you need to have the proper frame of mind. It is like planting; you need a fertile mind in order to realize the things you want.

Obviously some people have fertile minds and they realize their dreams with ease. The environment in which they grew up probably supported them in their endeavors. The rest of us on the other hand grew up in environments infested with poverty, oppression, slavery, apartheid, discrimination and racism. It is very difficult to have a fertile mind if you experienced any of these negative aspects of life. However this is not the end of life; it could as well be the beginning of a new life because you could overcome all these circumstances and as the Kama Sutra puts it, "the mortal gets what he or she wants"! This is the Universal Law and it doesn't depend on the whims and caprices of the cultural Gods; instead it depends on you!

There are many interventions that could help you to take back your life from the dictates of society including organized religion. I mention religion because for some it seems to be the last resort, but does religion really work? May be, but I have seen many people who are religious that fall to pieces when confronted with the challenges of life. In some cases they revert back to their former ways of life. The problem with some religious teachings is that they assure their followers that their God would protect them from the challenges of life. This is not true! Believers and non-believers are all subject to the challenges of life; no one is immune! However knowing yourself and using the proper intervention could make a difference.

Thus for religious people using practical solutions in addition to believing in their Gods could make a difference. On the other hand non-believers with positive minds could also attain the same results. As a non-believer you need to have an inquisitive mind and be responsible for your life. An Inquisitive Mind will help you to question everything under the sun; in this mind set there is no room for believing in any cultural God to give you the desires of your heart. Instead you believe in yourself and the Mystery that pervades the Universe which I call Universal Love (DIVINE). **Unlike the cultural Gods who promise what they can do for you if you believe, Universal Love has given you everything and it is your responsibility to simply go and get what you want! In this view you are not expecting anything from anyone and not even from the Cultural Gods and with that mind set you are able to triumph over many challenges!**

This is not to imply that the Cultural Gods are entirely useless; instead they are Cultural Icons that bring communities together and they could also listen to us when we need to share our problems and frustrations. However, contrary to popular beliefs, the Cultural Gods are neither omnipotent nor omniscient. All power belongs to the DIVINE, the Mystery that pervades the Universe

In spiritual practice the cultural Gods may also help us to cross the ocean of life but they are not the end. You need to focus your attention beyond the Cultural Gods if you want the total picture of the Universe.

I did not see a sacred space in our family home when I was growing up because at that time my family already converted to Christianity but the Sacred Space was one of the transformative things of my life after high school. The funny thing is that I learned about the sacred space from mystical organizations in the United

States instead of from my people. When my people converted to Christianity or when they were forced into Christianity they abandoned everything including their Sacred Spaces and their ancestors in favor of an invisible man who according to the missionaries would forgive their sins and give them eternal life. Now the question is how could the people who colonized and enslaved you give you anything good on this planet? If their message of eternal life is so great don't you think that they would only keep it for themselves? Religion is an instrument of control, oppression and exploitation and Christianity is the worst thing that happened to Africa!

The scientist has a lab and the producer has a studio but the human has no place to lay his head. Jesus said in the New Testament that "Foxes have dens and birds have nests, but the Son of Man has no place to lay his head" I am going to change that for you so that you have a place called home, your temporary home and that is the Sacred Space!

A Sacred Space is a sanctum, an altar, a sanctuary, a shrine, a place of reverence or a place of spiritual significance. It is usually a place set aside for prayer, thanksgiving, chanting or meditation. It is also a place for study and reflection. Now the question is why you should have a Sacred Space? Have you ever woken up in the morning and started using your cell phone or some gadget? Have you ever got out from bed and not knowing what to do with your life?

If you answered yes to both questions you are not alone, but you can change both. The sacred Place will help you to organize your life and later help you to create the circumstances of your life. The Sacred Place is also a place of refuge where you can feel safe, rejuvenated, and reassured after a day of problems and challenges. Further the Sanctum is a place you can associate with realizations, love, joy, motivation, success, peace, happiness, achievement, health and wellness! This was what our ancestors enjoyed in their

Sacred Spaces.

In the presentation on the Power of Myth on PBS, Bill Moyers
asked "What does it mean to have a sacred place?" Here is what
Joseph Campbell said: *A sacred place is a necessity for everybody.
You must have a room or a certain hour a day or so where you do
not know what was in the newspapers that morning, you don't
know who your friends are, you don't know what you owe to
anybody, you don't know what anybody owes you; but a place
where you can simply experience and bring forth what you are---
what you might be. This is the place of creative incubation. At first
you might find that nothing is happening there, but if you have a
sacred place and use it and take advantage of it something will
happen.*

As I said earlier I was first introduced to the Sacred Place by the
Alpha Mystery School in the seventies. Most, if not all Mystery
Schools introduce neophytes to the Sacred Place. The idea is to
help the student to study with concentration. The Sacred Place
makes it easy for anyone to sit, close the eyes and just be there.
You could be there for as long as you want. Sitting still and doing
nothing could be uncomfortable at the beginning but if you
consistently use your Sacred Place you would ask why no one told
you about the sacred place when you were born. It is that important
in your life!

I want you to note what Joseph Campbell said about the sacred
place: *This is the place of creative incubation. At first you might
find that nothing is happening there, but if you have a sacred place
and use it and take advantage of it something will happen.*

Yes, something could happen! The Sacred Place could help you to reconnect with yourself or with your life. You could almost handle anything when you reconnect with your life because the wisdom of life is within you. However you need to use your sacred place regularly in order to activate the wisdom within you. I cannot over emphasize the importance of the Sacred Place in your life. Thus if your life means anything to you I encourage you to setup, dedicate and use your Sacred Place? You could change your life forever!

The Sacred Place was part of my life until I got married. As I said earlier I was introduced to the sacred place by the "Alpha Mystery School". Generally I used it for meditation in the morning after cleaning up or after having a shower and in the evening before I went to sleep. I also used it for reflection, I mean to re-examine issues that I could not resolve more especially issues from work. I was working in the bank at the time. Lastly I used my sacred place for studying spiritual literature and the lessons from the "Alpha Mystery School". Thus the sanctum, as it is called in the mystery schools, was a present part of my life and it felt good.

When we got married my wife was a Christian and I did not want to introduce something that is alien to her at the beginning of our marriage so I packed everything and put them away. We lived happily for about 20 years. Then my life changed from one who has been happy all his life into one that became concerned about living. At the same time my sister passed on and it looked like I was really falling apart with negative thoughts and questioning my very existence. I could not see any reason to live if the people that meant a lot to me were dying. To say the least I was really depressed and hopeless for the first time in my life!

I became reactive and unhappy. It was clear that I was sick in my inner world. Meanwhile a thought flashed through my mind to setup my Sacred Place. After about a couple of months or so I summoned up the courage and looked for the boxes containing the materials. I did not set it up that day because there was no spare desk and I didn't have a table cloth. After about another month or so I acquired a desk and a table cloth and setup my Sacred Place again.

The moment I set it up my disposition changed. It seemed as though a positive energy passed through me. About two days after I setup the Sacred Place and used it our daughter came to my office to visit. The moment she saw me she said "Daddy you are happy". "Yes, I am happy", I said and I shared what I did to change my life.

I know we all have our ways of looking at things but in most cases we look at things from the perspective of the culture in which we grew up. The truth is that until you look at things from YOUR OWN WAY you'll continue to recycle the thoughts of your culture and possibly miss out on the blessings of life. I am trying my best to share a way of life that is not often talked about but this way of life could be the catalyst for a well adjusted life!

You have tried many things and failed in the past because they didn't come from you; they came from the society in which you grew up. Remember that mystics often leave the world to discover an inner world of peace, joy and happiness. What I am sharing is a way of life that puts you on the driver's seat. Thus instead of trying different things from different so-called gurus to find out what works; why not begin a way of life that works all the time! A way of life that surrounds you with love! A way of life that motivates you! A way of life that prospers you! A way of life that gives you peace! A way of life that makes you happy! Above all, a way of life that expands your consciousness! That way of life begins by setting up your Sacred Place and using it daily. And if you are wondering, that way of life was the way of life of your ancestors!

VOICE OF OUR ANCESTORS

African societies are built upon a worldview in which life is not limited to physical existence but stretches across visible and invisible dimensions. In this sacred continuum, the **ancestors** occupy a central place. They are the departed family members who continue to participate in the lives of the living, offering guidance, protection, and moral authority.

The **voice of the ancestors** is a vital concept in African thought. It is the way in which the departed speak to the living through ritual, memory, morality, and cultural institutions. Unlike Western conceptions of the dead as silent or absent, African traditions emphasize continuity: the dead are still part of the family and society.

Ancestors as Living People: In African cosmologies, the universe is relational. The Divine (often conceived as the High God) is distant but approachable through intermediaries like spirits, deities, and the ancestors.

- **The "Living Dead"**: The Kenyan theologian John Mbiti famously described the ancestors as the "Living Dead" meaning that they are physically dead but spiritually alive in memory and ritual.
- **Continuity of Family**: The Igbo concept of *ndi ichie* (ancestors) emphasizes that family ties do not end at death but extend into the spiritual realm.
- **Mediators**: Among the Shona of Zimbabwe, ancestors (*vadzimu*) act as intermediaries between the High God (*Mwari*) and the living, blessing crops, fertility, and health.

The ancestors' voice here is one of presence in the sense that they continue to exist as part of the community, reminding the living of the sacredness of family and lineage.

Significance of Rituals: A ritual is a repeated, formalized, symbolic act or sequence of actions performed for religious or secular purposes, such as a birthday ceremony, a religious service, or a life cycle ceremony. Rituals have a set structure and follow specific rules or traditions, often with symbolic meaning and significance that differs from ordinary actions. They can strengthen community bonds, mark important life transitions, and are found in almost all human societies.

Rituals hold profound significance by providing structure, meaning, and emotional grounding in both personal and communal life, serving to connect people, mark significant life transitions, transmit cultural knowledge, calm anxiety, and enable people to achieve better focus and performance. By transforming ordinary actions into meaningful, symbolic expressions, rituals help individuals and groups navigate challenges, reinforce social bonds, and integrate major changes in a shared and understandable way.

- **Libations**: In Akan society (Ghana), libations are poured to call the ancestors into family gatherings and decision-making. The spoken prayers involving invoking ancestral names carry the authority of ancestral voices.
- **Naming ceremonies**: Among the Yoruba, children are often named after ancestors, reflecting a belief that the ancestor's spirit continues in the child. The voice of the ancestor is thus heard in the very identity of the newborn.
- **Funerals**: In Zulu culture, funerals involve rituals that both honor the departed and ensure they become benevolent ancestors (*amadlozi*). The living ask the dead to continue speaking through dreams and blessings.
- **Divination**: Across Africa, diviners interpret signs, bones, and symbols as messages from ancestors. For example,

Yoruba *Ifá* divination is one way ancestors and deities reveal their voice.

Moral Authority: Ancestral moral authority is the concept that the values, customs, and traditions of one's forebears hold a special legitimacy and provide a basis for moral reasoning. This form of authority is unwritten and is derived from a community's long-standing history, rather than from formal legal or bureaucratic structures.

- **Proverbs**: Many African proverbs are regarded as the voice of ancestral wisdom. For instance, the Igbo say, *"What an elder sees sitting, a child cannot see standing,"* emphasizing that ancestral wisdom surpasses youthful ignorance.
- **Taboos and customs**: Violating taboos often invokes ancestral disapproval. Among the Shona, breaking moral codes risks illness or misfortune as a sign of ancestral displeasure.
- **Ethical compass**: The Akan say, *"The clan is like a cluster of trees—if you cut one, the rest feel it."* This ancestral teaching emphasizes solidarity and warns against selfishness.

In African societies, morality is not only about DIVINE law but also about honoring the ancestors who watch over behavior. Their voice acts as conscience.

Ancestral Voice in Leadership: Ancestral voice in leadership refers to the concept of retrieving and applying deep, body-embodied wisdom from past generations to guide contemporary decision-making and create a unique path forward. This intergenerational knowledge, particularly from Indigenous traditions, is informed by values such as community, place-based continuity, and ethical conduct, and fosters a leadership style focused on collective benefit and spiritual connection, rather than solely individual or corporate interests.

- **Chieftaincy**: Among the Akan, chiefs are seen as "sitting on the ancestral stool," symbolizing that their authority is derived from ancestors. Decisions are made in their name.
- **Council of elders**: In many traditions, elders are regarded as the "living voices" of ancestors. The Igbo *ndichie* (council of elders) consult the ancestors before making judgments.
- **Zulu leadership**: Zulu kings invoke the ancestors during national rituals, ensuring that leadership aligns with ancestral blessing.
- **Sanctions**: Leaders who fail to uphold justice risk losing ancestral support, which may manifest in drought, defeat, or social unrest.

Here, the voice of the ancestors is a political force, ensuring that leadership remains accountable to tradition and cosmic order.

Ancestral Cultural Understanding: Ancestral cultural understanding is the comprehension and appreciation of the history, traditions, language, values, and beliefs of one's own or other ancestors. This understanding fosters a stronger sense of identity and belonging, preserves cultural heritage through practices and language, and promotes tolerance and a deeper connection to the global human experience. It can be achieved through genealogical research, intergenerational communication, and participation in culturally-based practices and ceremonies. Through memory, ritual performance, and cultural practice, the ancestors continue to shape the collective voice of society.

- **Oral traditions**: Stories, myths, and epics are remembered as ancestral voices. For instance, the Yoruba *Oriki* (praise poetry) invokes ancestors to affirm identity and history.
- **Festivals**: In Nigeria, the Igbo *New Yam Festival* honors both the earth and the ancestors, affirming cultural continuity.

- **Genealogies**: Among the Shona, reciting family lineages is an act of listening to the ancestors' voice, ensuring no name is forgotten.
- **Egungun masquerades**: Among the Yoruba, masked dancers embody ancestral spirits, speaking to the community with the authority of the ancestors.

In African society, the ancestors are not silent. Their voice is alive in ritual, morality, politics, and culture. They guide the living, sanction leaders, protect families, and preserve cultural identity. The ancestors' voice ensures that the living remain connected to their past while preparing the way for future generations.

To honor the ancestors is to honor continuity, memory, and sacred order. To ignore them is to risk losing identity and balance. The African conviction is clear: the dead do not disappear; they speak—and their voice is the foundation of society's spiritual and moral strength.

Setting up Your Sacred Place
Setting up your Sacred Place and using it is one of the transformative things you can do for yourself and your family. If you live in a room you can use a corner of the room for your sacred place. If you are a family you might need a bigger space with a table and chairs and a place for your ancestors.

Do you have a corner in your bedroom, family room, living room, child's room, in an attic or in the basement? If you do, here are some of the things you need to setup your Sacred Place. If you do not have a corner at the moment, still stay with me because you can also use this information to setup your Inner Sacred Place. I will list the things that I use in my Sacred Place.

1. Desk and chair.
2. Table cloth to cover the surface. Choose your favorite color. I use white.
3. Picture of a saint, a savior, an angel, wedding photo, family photo, parent's photo, your favorite photo. I

first used the Healing Christ but as my awareness evolved I replaced it with the picture of the Buddha in serene contemplation which I later changed to my own favorite photo. Later, I decided to replace my photo with the image of Universal Love. Thus the image you use may depend on the level of your awareness and of course your preferences.

4. Picture of a sunset, sun rise, river, flowers, trees, plants, squirrel, pet, snow capped mountain. I love flowers.

5. Candles, candleholders, incense, clock, incense burner, lighter, candle snuffer, spiritual clothing like a graduation gown and a mirror. You can use a white graduation gown. I have a black graduation gown with golden yellow stripes.

6. Symbol of spiritual significance like the cross. You can use any type of cross. I use the cross of UNISM

7. Sacred Texts, diary, pen, writing pad. Be prepared for the inspiration that could really change your life! For sacred texts I use the Bhagavad Gita, Upanishads, Tao Te Ching, the Tanakh, the New Testament, the Qur'an, the Rig Veda, the Dhammapada, the Analects of Confucius and the Universal Holy Book. I used most of the famous sacred texts because I was studying them and I usually study them during my daily meditation periods. At the moment I do not use any of them.

8. Music player and spiritual music CDs. You can use spiritual music to set the mood more especially when you wake up in the morning before you begin your spiritual practice.

I want you to know that this is your life and you came with a clean slate to write on it. Would you write what you learned from your culture or would you write your experiences? The choice is yours! The book, Unto Thee I Grant teaches us that "the noblest employment of the mind of man is the study of the works of his creator". You do not study by recycling the experiences of others; you need a firsthand experience and that experience begins with knowing who you are!

Now the question is how do you find out who you really are? To answer this question we need to learn from the Buddha and similar people. Without going into the history of the Buddha and the others we can just learn to sit in one place and do nothing. That was essentially what they did.

Sacred Place Texts are the texts you want to use during your spiritual practice. At my level of awareness I can say that you really do not need any texts because whatever text you choose is going to be someone else's experience. However, most if not all of us grew up with texts that mean a lot to us. In the same way society tells us that we need the cultural Gods and we become used to them. The truth is that you do not need the texts and you do not need the Gods. However if you are struggling with a personal problem the Gods could come in handy because you believe that they have powers. Thus, you can use them to help you to solve your problems. It is like using a boat to cross a river; the moment you cross the river you do not need the boat anymore. If you carry the boat with you it becomes an obstruction!

I know society has made a case for believing in a cultural God for the rest of your life and billions of people do so today. The truth is that your God is your obstruction to life. The Gods are limited; they do not go along with progress more especially progress about human rights. If there were no human laws to protect our rights many religious people who follow the words of their Gods would stone homosexuals to death. This is where cultural Gods become obstructions! You are here to love without conditions as the

DIVINE loves you without conditions! The Gods only love you with conditions. Wake up because you were not born into conditions!

I am aware that most of us need the sacred texts because we believe that we are sinners or we are fallen. I also believed that way at one point in my life. That was why I used the sacred texts to help me to cross to the other side of the river. My years of practice and study finally paid off. I no longer believe that I am a sinner or I am fallen and I no longer need the cultural Gods or the sacred texts because I now embrace the DIVINE! However if you believe in your sacred texts and your cultural Gods it is all right to use them.

What are your favorite texts or what kinds of texts do you want to use in your Sacred Place? I mean texts that could inspire you or help you to reflect. I used the Bible when I began my spiritual practice. I learned about more sacred texts later in my life and used the Upanishads, the Bhagavad Gita, the Tao Te Ching, the Dammapada, the Tanakh, the Qur'an, the Rig Veda and the Analects of Confucius. But before we discuss the Sacred Place Texts you need I want to take a moment and encourage you to start collecting the materials for setting up your Sacred Place.

Once again here is the list of materials you need to setup your physical Sacred Place: Desk, chair, tablecloth, sanctum master picture, candles, candleholders, incense, digital clock, incense burner, lighter, candle snuffer, spiritual clothing, mirror, symbol of spiritual significance like the cross, sanctum texts, diary, pen, writing pad, music player and spiritual music CDs.

Take your time and do not rush but your journey toward a fulfilling life begins with setting up your Sacred Place! If you have no purpose in life, if you want to take back your life, if you want to experience living your life from within, if you want to be on the driver's seat of your life, if you want to be fulfilled and if you want to be happy I encourage you to begin to gather the materials you need to setup your Sacred Place today!

I specially encourage young men and women to consider setting up a Sacred Place to prepare you for the challenges of life in your later years more especially when you get married and begin to raise a family or when you become the president of your corporation or when you become the president of your country. These positions require emotional and spiritual maturity. Sometimes life takes us by surprise. Spiritual practice prepares you mostly for the surprises of life! Begin a way of life that works all the time!

As I said earlier I used the major sacred texts during my sanctum meditations. I do not read all of them at the same time and I may not even read any of them during my practice. It all depends on the inspiration for that moment. However I am not limited to the sacred texts. I also use other texts like the Future of an illusion by Sigmund Freud, Creative Mind and Success by Earnest Holmes, the Secret by Rhonda Byrne, A Separate Reality by Carlos Castenada, the Seat of the Soul by Gary Zukav, Unto Thee I Grant, Psycho Cybernetics by Maxwell Maltz, The Seven Spiritual Laws of Success by Deepak Chopra, Think and Grow Rich by Napoleon Hill and In Tune with the infinite by Ralph Waldo Trine.

This is just a few of the books I like but I have over 500 books in my library. What I am saying is that you are not limited in your choice of books. The goal is knowledge and the more you know the more you understand. The more you understand the more you love without conditions. The more you love without conditions the more you become part of the CREATURE FAMILY.

As I said earlier I used the Healing Christ when I started my Sacred Place practices. Remember that the purpose of a cultural God is to help you to cross the river to the other side. As I became more aware of my environment I replaced the Healing Christ with the Buddha in serene contemplation. I changed to the Buddha because he appears better suited for the spiritual practices. Later I changed the Buddha to use my own photo. Lately I now use the image of Universal Love! If I can predict the progression the end of the practice is to use NOTHING!

A Sacred Place Master is the image you place before you during your spiritual practice. Your Sacred Place Master could be a Savior, a God, a Bodhisattva, a Buddha or none of them. It is your choice. I have included the masters because most of us grew up with believing in cultural Gods. Thus it seems easy to incorporate them into our spiritual practices. Here are a few of the popular images.

Yemoja
Yemoja also known as Yemaya is an Orisha Goddess from the Yoruba religion. She was transported to the new world during the Trans-Atlantic slave trade and manifests in different forms in the Americas. Yemoja is the ultimate protectress; she protects her children and specially favors women with respect to love, conception, childbirth, parenting and healing.

Lakshmi
Lakshmi is a Hindu Goddess of wealth, fortune and prosperity but she is also an important Goddess in Jainism. She also protects her devotees from sickness and adversity.

Saraswathi
Saraswathi is the Hindu Goddess of knowledge, music, art, wisdom, and learning. She is the mother of the Vedas and she represents intelligence, consciousness, cosmic knowledge, creativity, education, enlightenment, power, and "divine knowledge." She is also the Goddess of speech and associated with fertility and purification.

Tara

Tara is a female bodhisattva in Mahayana Buddhism but she also appears as a female Buddha in Vajrayana Buddhism or Tibetan Buddhism. She is the Goddess of Peace and Protection but also appears in different colors with different functions:

- Green Tara is associated with compassion,
- White Tara is associated with compassion, long life, healing and serenity.
- Red Tara is associated with attracting good things to her devotees.
- Black Tara is associated with power
- Yellow Tara is associated with wealth and prosperity.
- Blue Tara is associated with the transmutation of anger

Krishna

Krishna is the eighth incarnation of Lord Vishnu in Hinduism but we mostly associate him with the Bhagavad Gita where he encourages Arjuna to fight in the battle between the Kurus and the Pandavas. He is often depicted as the one God and as an Avatara or incarnation. He is considered as the God of compassion tenderness, love and forgiveness.

Christ

Christ is the Christian savior and messiah. He is also known as Jesus of Nazareth. He is mostly depicted as the Healing Christ, the Crucified Christ or the Holy Christ. He is associated with forgiveness, manifestation, transformation, healing, love and peace.

Avalokiteshvara

Avalokiteshvara is a celestial Bodhisattva. He is the Lord who looks down with compassion on all beings. He is known as Chenrezik in Tibet and as Quanyin, a female Bodhisattva in China. He is associated with infinite compassion and love for all beings.

Buddha

Buddha is the founder of Buddhism. His name is Siddhartha Gautama. He is mostly known for his serene contemplation pose but he has also been depicted as Medicine Buddha (Healing Buddha), wrathful Buddha or the Buddha as the union of male and female. He is mostly associated with compassion and wisdom.

Amitabha

Amitabha is a celestial Buddha. He is also known as Amida or Amitayus. He is the Buddha of immeasurable Light and Life. He is a savior and also associated with compassion.

Vishnu

Vishnu is a great Hindu God. He is the preserver and protector of the universe. He descends to the earth at critical times to restore righteousness. So far he has come to the earth nine times and will come again toward the end of this age. He is often associated with creation, liberation, preservation, protection and strength.

Shiva

Shiva is another great Hindu God. He is the creator, destroyer and transformer of the universe. He is often depicted as the half woman Lord, the Lord of the dance and the Great Yogi. He is associated with compassion, power and triumph over the ego.

These are by no means all the cultural Gods, Saviors, Bodhisattvas, or Buddhas. You are free to check out as many Gods as you can. If you want to resolve a personal problem I encourage you to choose the one that is most likely to help you to resolve the problem. This means that you need to know their specializations. For instance if you want to give birth to children you may choose Goddess Tara, or Quanyin and if you want wealth and prosperity you need Goddess Lakshmi

A great lesson to learn about the Gods is that they are all within us.

Thus meditating on a God or Praying to a God helps us to activate the powers we need to resolve our problems. Thus it is very important for you to take time to study each of them and choose the ones that could bring out the best in you.

If you have resolved your personal problems and want more from the practice I encourage you to begin your spiritual practices with the image of the Buddha in serene contemplation but it all depends on the image that appeals to you. In this respect I will be more inclined to use the image of an ancestor than the image of a foreign God.

The next stage of the practice is for you to replace your sanctum image with your own photo! The main purpose of the Cultural Gods is to help us to cross to the other side of the ocean. A time will come when you will realize that the Infinite is also within you! When you know that the Mystery of the Universe is within you there is nothing higher to be known!

As I said earlier the end of the journey is when you realize that you don't need any image; in other words you need NOTHING. Reaching this state of NOTHINGNESS is the whole purpose of spiritual practice! At this point you become one with the Universe!

Setting up Your Family Sacred Place

A family sacred place is a location within a home, or a designated corner, that a family sets aside and infuses with spiritual significance for activities like prayer, study, reflection, and fostering faith. It's a personalized, intimate space that encourages a connection to the DIVINE and serves as a refuge for spiritual practice and emotional security, often marked by meaningful objects and rituals.

Common objects found in a family sacred place, often called a home altar or shrine, vary widely depending on the family's faith, culture, and individual beliefs. Many items are included to represent the family's spiritual values and to serve as a focus for prayer and reflection. For a greater percentage of families who have sacred places the common objects include a sacred text, a religious symbol like the cross, a religious icon like a photo of Jesus, Krishna, Buddha or Yemoja, a prayer book, rosaries, holy water or oil, incense, photographs of Ancestors and other deceased family members. The family Sacred Place may also include rocks, plants, seashells, candles, journals, a table and chairs.

My thoughts about a Family Sacred Place is to avoid clutter. Have a table and chairs and have a place for your ancestors and other deceased members of the family. Your ancestors are more important than any foreign cultural Gods! If you do not have photographs of your ancestors and the other deceased members of your family you could have them drawn by a professional. Your Family Sacred Place could as well be your Family Spiritual Center where you meet at least once a week for study, meditation and worship.

AFRICAN SPIRITUAL VISION

For centuries, Western anthropologists and colonial powers dismissed African spiritual systems as "primitive animism," "paganism," or "fetishism," terms laden with pejorative connotations and a fundamental misunderstanding of their sophistication. The African Spiritual Vision is, in reality, a metaphysical and philosophical system that provides a complete explanation of existence, a moral and ethical code, and a practical guide for living in harmony with the visible and invisible worlds. It is a worldview that is fundamentally life-affirming, community-oriented, and immanently spiritual, perceiving the DIVINE not as a distant entity that judges people but as an active force permeating all of creation.

Core Philosophical Pillars of the African Spiritual Vision
While immense diversity exists among the thousands of ethnic groups in Africa, several foundational principles form a common thread uniting the African spiritual landscape including the interconnectedness of all things, the centrality of community, the presence of the Ancestors and the sacredness of the environment

The Interconnectedness of All Things: The most fundamental tenet is the absence of a rigid separation between the sacred and the secular, the spiritual and the physical. All reality is viewed as a single, interconnected whole. The universe is a vast, dynamic network of relationships and forces. This means a rock, a river, a tree, an animal, a human, and an ancestor are all part of a continuous, sacred existence. This principle is encapsulated in the Southern African concept of Ubuntu, often translated as "I am because we are." The individual's humanity is inextricably tied to the community of both the living and the dead.

The Centrality of Community: Life is the ultimate value, and this

56

life is understood as a vital force or energy. The goal of human existence is not to escape the world but to strengthen, protect, and increase this vital force within oneself, one's family, and one's community. Community, therefore, is the crucible of life. The individual finds identity, purpose, and protection within the collective. Harmony within the community is paramount, as discord diminishes the collective vital force.

The Presence of Ancestors: Ancestral veneration is a cornerstone of the African Spiritual Vision. Ancestors are not merely "dead" relatives; they are present in spiritual form and are active members of the community. They are guardians of tradition, moral exemplars, and intermediaries between the living and the higher divinities. Proper remembrance through libations, prayers, and offerings ensures their continued blessing, guidance, and protection. Neglect can lead to their displeasure, manifesting as misfortune or illness.

The Sacredness of the Environment: The natural world is not a mere resource to be exploited but a manifestation of the DIVINE. Specific landscapes like mountains, rivers, forests, and specific animals are often seen as abodes of spirits or gods. This fosters a deep-seated ethic of environmental respect and conservation. The Earth is often viewed as a mother goddess (e.g., Ala in Igbo tradition, Asase Yaa in Akan tradition), whose fertility and well-being are essential for human survival.

Structure of the African Spiritual Hierarchy

African spiritual systems are deeply rooted in a complex hierarchy of spiritual entities, ranging from the DIVINE to Deities, ancestral spirits, and spirits of nature. This hierarchy reflects the worldview that the universe is a layered and interconnected realm, where spiritual forces influence daily life, morality, and community well-being. Understanding this hierarchy reveals how African societies organize their spiritual life, assign roles to different entities, and manifest their beliefs through rituals, ceremonies, and social structures.

The DIVINE: The DIVINE or Supreme Being is at the apex of the hierarchy. IT is the one transcendent, omnipotent, omnipresent Supreme GOD, the creator and source of all life. The DIVINE is known by various names across the continent: including Olodumare (Yoruba), Chukwu (Igbo), Nyame (Akan), Umvelinqangi (Zulu), Ngai (Kikuyu), Tamuno (Ijaw) and Amma (Dogon). The DIVINE is beyond human comprehension. It is said to be the creator of all existence including the Gods and Spirits. It is often revered through rituals, prayers, and offerings, though direct worship may be limited or mediated through subordinate spirits

Divinities & Deities (Gods): Acting as ministers or emissaries of the Supreme God are a pantheon of divinities. They personify natural forces, cosmic principles, and aspects of human endeavor. The Divinities include Nature deities, Social Deities and Healing deities. The nature deities include Gods of Rivers, Mountains, Rain, War, Justice, Fertility, or Storms. Among the Yoruba Orishas, Ogun is the God of War, Yemoja, the Goddess of Fertility and Family; Sango, the God of Thunder and Justice and Oshun is the God of Love. Social Deities are associated with kingship, justice, or the well being of the community. Healing Deities are responsible for health and medicine. The Divinities are often anthropomorphic but embody specific natural or moral principles. They are approachable through rituals, sacrifices, and offerings and play vital roles in daily life, rituals, and festivals.

Ancestral Spirits: Ancestors occupy a central position in the spiritual hierarchy. They are the spirits of deceased relatives who have achieved harmony and moral righteousness. They act as guardians, guides, and protectors of their descendants. Their voices are invoked in rituals, dreams, and divination. They serve as mediators between the living and the higher divine realm, enforce moral conduct within families and communities, and their ongoing influence sustains social order and cultural continuity.

Nature & Elemental Spirits: Nature Spirits include spirits of rivers, forests, rocks, trees, animals, winds, and other natural elements. They are often regarded as manifestations or servants of higher spirits. Respect and rituals are performed to appease or honor these spirits. Mostly they influence natural phenomena and individual fortunes. They are usually associated with specific sacred sites or objects. And they can be benevolent or malevolent depending on the context.

Key Practices of African Spirituality

African spirituality is a rich tapestry of beliefs and rituals that emphasize harmony between humans, nature, ancestors, and the divine. Unlike organized religions with fixed doctrines, African spiritual practices are diverse, community-centered, and deeply rooted in cultural traditions. These practices serve to maintain spiritual balance, uphold moral values, and strengthen social bonds.

Rituals & Sacrifice: Rituals are prescribed actions that maintain balance and communication between the visible and invisible worlds. Sacrifice (offering of food, drink, or animals) is not about appeasing a vengeful deity but about giving back energy to sustain the spiritual forces that sustain humanity. It is an act of exchange and communion.

Divination: Divination is a sophisticated system for seeking knowledge and guidance from the spiritual realm. It is used to diagnose the causes of misfortune, prescribe remedies, and understand the will of the divinities and ancestors. The Ifá system of the Yoruba, involving a skilled Babalawo and a complex corpus of poetry (Odu), is one of the most renowned and intricate divination systems in the world.

Ancestor Worship and Veneration: One of the central practices in African spirituality is reverence for ancestors. Regular offerings of food, drinks (libations), and prayers are made to ancestors at family shrines or sacred sites. Dreams, divination, and omens serve as channels through which ancestors communicate guidance or warnings. Annual ancestor festivals and rituals reinforce the ongoing relationship between the living and the dead. Respecting ancestors entails moral living, honesty, and community service, as ancestors are seen as moral exemplars and protectors.

Rituals and Ceremonies: Rituals are vital for maintaining spiritual harmony and marking significant life events. Life Cycle ceremonies such as birth rites, coming-of-age ceremonies, marriages, and funerals are elaborate rituals that connect individuals with spiritual forces and community identity. Traditional healers (herbalists, diviners, spiritual doctors) perform rituals to cure illnesses, which are often viewed as spiritual imbalances or curses. Cleansing rituals involve water, herbs, or symbolic objects to purify individuals or spaces from negative energies.

Offerings and Sacrifices: Offering sacrifices is a common practice to honor spirits, deities, and ancestors. Animals such as goats, chickens, or bulls are offered during festivals or significant events to seek favor or appease spirits (we should put an end to animal sacrifices because like us the animals enjoy living). Fruits, grains, and traditional dishes are presented at shrines, altars, or sacred sites. Pouring liquid (water, wine, or traditional brews) on the ground or altars symbolizes respect and communication with spiritual forces.

Sacred Sites and Objects: Sacred spaces and objects are central to African spiritual practices. Natural sites are considered dwelling places of spirits or deities, and are often preserved and protected. Family or community altars are dedicated to ancestors or spirits, and decorated with offerings and symbols. Masks, talismans, charms, and relics imbued with spiritual power, are used in rituals and ceremonies.

Music, Dance, and Festivals: Music and dance are not mere entertainment but spiritual expressions. Sacred Songs and Drumming are used to invoke spirits, accompany rituals, or communicate with ancestors. Dance movements are symbolic, representing stories, spiritual messages, or honoring deities. Festivals provide opportunities for community gatherings that celebrate seasons, harvests, or ancestors, reinforcing cultural identity and spiritual harmony.

Moral and Ethical Practices: African spirituality emphasizes living in harmony with others and the environment. The Ubuntu Philosophy or the principle "I am because we are" promotes compassion, community support, and mutual respect. Rituals and taboos protect natural elements, reinforcing sustainable living. Upholding truth, honesty, hospitality, and social responsibility is seen as spiritual duty.

 Healing and Spiritual Medicine: Healing practices blend spiritual rituals with herbal medicine. Herbalists and Diviners use plants, charms, and rituals to diagnose and cure ailments believed to be caused by spiritual imbalance or malevolent spirits. Spiritual Cleansing involves using rituals to remove curses, evil spirits, or negative energies affecting health or fortune.

African spirituality encompasses a wide array of practices that foster spiritual harmony, social cohesion, and cultural identity. Its key practices—ancestor veneration, rituals, offerings, divination, sacred sites, music, and moral conduct—are deeply intertwined with daily life and community values. These practices serve not only to connect individuals with spiritual forces but also to sustain the moral fabric of society and respect for the natural world. Recognizing and understanding these practices offers profound insight into the rich spiritual heritage of Africa, emphasizing a worldview rooted in harmony, reverence, and interconnectedness

African Spiritual Experiences
The Impact of Foreign Religions: The arrival of Islam and Christianity, often through trade, colonization, and missionary activities, posed a significant challenge to indigenous African spirituality. **For instance** missionary and colonial influences often labeled African spiritual systems as "pagan," leading to the suppression and loss of indigenous rituals, shrines, and oral traditions.

The veneration of ancestors—central to African spirituality—was replaced by the worship of foreign deities, weakening the ancestral and communal foundation of spiritual life. Conversion to foreign religions often required rejection of traditional values, creating psychological and cultural disconnection from indigenous identity. New moral codes introduced by Christianity and Islam redefined gender roles, family structure, and social hierarchy, often contradicting African communal ethics. Many Africans today live in tension between traditional spirituality and imported religious doctrines, creating inner conflict and identity fragmentation.

Both Christianity and Islam presented themselves as the one true faith, destined to replace "pagan" or "heathen" African beliefs. This theological stance justified the suppression of indigenous practices. Deities (Orishas, Vodun, Abosom) were re-cast as "demons." Ancestral veneration was labeled "witchcraft." Sacred groves and shrines were destroyed or abandoned. Rituals were seen as "savage" or "devil worship." The active suppression led to the erosion of spiritual knowledge, as elders were silenced, and younger generations were educated in mission schools to despise their own heritage.

Colonial administrations often worked hand-in-hand with missionaries. Adopting Christianity could provide access to Western education, jobs, and social mobility, creating a practical incentive to abandon indigenous faiths. The linear, time-bound worldview of Abrahamic religions (with a creation and an end-time) often replaced the cyclical, community-centric worldview of African spirituality, which was deeply tied to the land and the seasons. Many indigenous practices were outlawed, forcing them underground.

Missionaries sometimes used native words for "God" (e.g., Nyame in Akan, Olodumare in Yoruba) to translate the Christian God, which created a point of connection but also flattened the complex understanding of a Supreme Being who works through intermediaries. African Initiated Churches emerged, blending Christian theology with African cultural elements like prophecy, healing, drumming, and dance, representing an early form of resistance and adaptation.

The Phenomenon of Syncretism: Syncretism is the blending of different religious beliefs and practices. It was a key survival strategy for African spirituality and has resulted in the creation of vibrant new religious expressions, particularly in the African Diaspora.

Enslaved Africans in the Americas, forced to practice Catholicism, secretly worshipped their Orishas, Vodun, and Nkisi by identifying them with Catholic saints. For example: The Yoruba Orisha **Shangó** was syncretized with **Saint Barbara** (both associated with thunder and power). The Vodun spirit **Papa Legba** (gatekeeper) was syncretized with **Saint Peter** (keeper of the keys to heaven). This allowed the core theology and practices to continue under the guise of acceptable Christian worship.

This syncretism gave birth to entirely new, sophisticated religions that are now practiced by millions: **Vodou (Haiti):** A blend of West African Vodun, Fon, and Kongo beliefs with Roman Catholicism. **Santería/Lucumí (Cuba):** A blend of Yoruba religion and Spanish Catholicism. **Candomblé (Brazil):** A blend of Yoruba, Fon, and Bantu beliefs with some Catholic influences. And other examples include Palo Mayombe, Umbanda, and Obeah.

While syncretism preserved the traditions, it also created internal tensions. Purists within these traditions often seek to "de-syncretize" and return to the African source, removing the Christian layers they see as a necessary but temporary mask.

Contemporary Resurgence and Global Influence: Today, there is a powerful resurgence of interest in African traditional spirituality. This is driven by Cultural Reclamation, Ecological Wisdom and Holistic Wellbeing. Cultural Reclamation is a desire to decolonize the mind and reconnect with pre-colonial identities and heritage. Ecological Wisdom centers on the sacredness of nature and offers a crucial alternative to exploitative environmental models. And Holistic Wellbeing focuses on community, ancestral connection, and ritual to address modern ailments of alienation, anxiety, and emptiness. Traditions like Ifá, Vodou, and Candomblé have gained followers worldwide, influencing global spirituality, psychology, and the arts.

As African nations gained independence, there was a concerted effort to reclaim pre-colonial cultural and spiritual identities as a source of pride and authenticity, countering the narrative of European/Arab superiority. Africans realized the impact of narratives on human consciousness and started building organizations to counter Western and Arab narratives. Movements like "Afrocentricity" placed Africa at the center of historical and cultural analysis, revitalizing interest in Kemetic (Ancient Egyptian) and other traditional African spiritual systems. Diasporic Identity and Roots Tourism help people in the diaspora to trace their ancestry to specific regions in Africa which has fueled a desire to connect with the spiritual traditions of their ancestors.

Pilgrimages help People from the Americas and Europe to travel to West Africa and other regions as spiritual tourists to be initiated into traditions like Ifá, Vodun, and other African religions. Digital Access provides Africans everywhere to access knowledge that was once secret or inaccessible. Websites, social media groups, and online stores for spiritual supplies have created global communities of practitioners. References in music (e.g., Beyoncé's *Lemonade*), film, and fashion have brought symbols of Orisha worship, Vodun, and other traditions into the mainstream, sparking curiosity and reducing stigma. Many are drawn to African spirituality's inherent respect for nature, seeing it as a more ecologically balanced worldview compared to the exploitative nature of industrial modernity. Systems like Ifá divination offer personalized guidance and a framework for understanding one's destiny (Ori), which appeals to individuals seeking meaning outside of mainstream religions.

An Enduring Vision for a Connected World

The African Spiritual Vision is not a relic of the past but a living, breathing, and dynamic worldview. It offers a profound understanding of life as a web of sacred relationships. Its core tenets—the unity of existence, the reverence for ancestors, the sacredness of community and nature—provide timeless insights. In an era of global crises, from environmental degradation to social fragmentation, this vision presents a compelling path forward. It reminds us that human flourishing is inseparable from the health of our communities, our connection to our heritage, and our respectful relationship with the natural world. The unbroken circle linking the unborn, the living, the ancestors, and the cosmos endures, offering a vision of harmony, resilience, and profound meaning for all of humanity.

The African Spiritual Path to Life
Christians have the Ten Commandments, Buddhists have the
Precepts, Hindus have the Dharma and Muslims have the Shariah.
Africans on the other hand have the Twelve Paths to Life as
follows:

1. Honor the DIVINE all the days of your life.
2. Honor your ancestors in truth, and pass their wisdom to
   future generations.
3. Honor your family, for it is the first temple of the DIVINE.
4. Protect the weak, the widow, the orphan, and the stranger.
5. Cherish the earth, for it is your mother and your dwelling.
6. Acknowledge the Spirit within you and cultivate your inner
   power.
7. Seek Wisdom and Knowledge, for you are the new LIGHT.
8. Speak truth, and avoid telling lies for as long as you live.
9. Share what you have, for greed destroys community.
10. Celebrate life with the help of rituals, songs and dances.
11. Do No Harm to Any Soul or Spirit
12. Have a vision for your life and work with Purpose and
    Diligence in order to realize your dreams.

PERSONAL RESPONSIBILITY

So far I have tried to state the reasons why the writing of the African Testament of GOD is important and necessary. In the process I may have used words and phrases that called your beliefs and your very existence to question. I have purposely done this to open the door for critical thinking and reflection. It is no longer safe or in your best interest to accept whatever society tells you. They parade their Gods as Universal Gods and ignore the Almighty GOD. They promulgate their sacred texts and ignore the real sacred text of the GOD of the Universe. All these are for the sake of world dominance but that day will never come because the Almighty GOD never created any nation, race of people or religion to dominate the world. It is therefore very important that you take a stand on FREEDOM, EQUALITY and HUMNAN RIGHTS.

In the United States the Supreme Court guarantees the Freedom for same sex couples to marry but some sacred texts teach the stoning to death of homosexuals. If you believed your sacred text and killed a homosexual you could be imprisoned or be killed. The Almighty GOD does not tell anyone to abuse, deceive, discriminate, kill or enslave GOD's creatures. GOD loves all creatures without conditions. If you abuse, kill, deceive, discriminate or enslave anyone, it is your choice and you must live with the consequences. However the Almighty GOD knows that you are not entirely to be blamed for your wrong choices and GOD always forgives. You must take responsibility for your actions and that responsibility begins with critical thinking and reflection. In short you have a moral duty to re-think the world because that is the only thing that guarantees continued renewal and progress in life!

There was a time in my life when I got all my answers from my foreign sacred text, the Bible. I remember always quoting my foreign sacred text each time people wanted my opinion and I even quoted my foreign sacred text during my Ph.D. oral examination. That was how lost I was! But after my breakthrough I re-examined some of the conflicts of my life again. One of them was about homosexuals and the other was the famous Heinz dilemma in psychology. I still feel ashamed each time I remember my answers more especially the one in my Ph.D. oral examination. However if you are willing to learn your consciousness could change and you might see the possibilities in life.

In this re-examination it is important to note that my foreign sacred text is no longer the word of GOD. The word of GOD is spread in the Universe and no text can contain it! Thus in such situations when you want direction from GOD you do not search the sacred texts for answers; the natural thing to do is to meditate on the issue and the Almighty GOD will show you the way! I meditated on the subject for three days. At the end of my meditation and reflection I realized that the Almighty GOD also loves homosexuals without conditions and it is therefore not my place to discriminate against them. Thus instead of referring to your sacred text as the word of GOD and hiding under it, take personal responsibility for all your actions. **Sacred texts stop the conversation but in this world we want to continue the conversation because it is our only hope for peace and understanding.**

Heinz Dilemma was a questionnaire for one of my classes during my masters program at Miami University, Oxford, Ohio, USA. We were studying Lawrence Kohlberg's stages of moral development and the professor used the story to determine our stages of moral development. According to the story a woman was near death but there was one drug that could save her life. A druggist manufactured the drug for about $200 but he was charging ten times what the drug cost him to produce. Heinz, the woman's husband, went to everyone he knew to borrow the money but he could only come up with $1000. Heinz went to the druggist and told him to accept the $1000 and allow him to pay the remaining $1000 in installments but the druggist refused Heinz's offer.

Meanwhile Heinz only has two choices: to steal the drug or to let his wife die? And the question they asked us was "what would you do if you were Heinz?

For me it was easy because my foreign sacred text tells me "Thou shall not steal", which translates into the answer that I would let my wife die. But after my breakthrough I re-examined Heinz's dilemma and decided that I would steal the drug to save my wife. What has changed? Instead of hiding under a sacred text I took personal responsibility and with the knowledge of the consequences of stealing. When our son was about 5 years old I shared Heinz's dilemma with him and asked him what he would do if he were Heinz? He said that he would steal the drug! What is the difference between my son and I? My son has not been influenced by society and has his own ideas of right and wrong instead of from a sacred text. In other words he thinks for himself! My ideas of right and wrong on the other hand were from a sacred text; I had no thoughts of my own. I really felt less developed than our 5-year old son when he shared his thoughts on the subject. Society prefers those who do not think but if you love your life and you want to develop yourself you must think!

Now some of you might be conflicted with lots of questions and I understand but for now simply be still and do nothing. Here are some hypothetical questions and their answers regarding the African Testament of GOD and African Spirituality:

Should I leave my Foreign Religion Now?
This book was written to inform and to invite. It was not intended to force anyone to do what they do not want to do. In the main the book calls for reflection in the light of the life of Africans and members of the African Diaspora. To leave or not to leave a foreign religion is a choice you must make after considering all the facts. The facts of colonization, the facts of slavery, the facts of Apartheid, the facts of discrimination, the facts of racism and the facts of white encounter with Africans.

You also need to consider what would replace the foreign religion when you leave. This book recommends a Family African Religion to bring the family together and to sing praises to your ancestors instead of foreign Gods irrespective of their promises and threats. **Please do not leave your foreign religion without a substitute** because the after effects is similar to one who withdraws from a drug use without proper medical attention. And do not take the withdrawal effects from religion for granted; I had a hole in heart when I fired my Christian God. The hole only got sealed after I read the Upanishads.

What should I do if I do not feel that my religion is Foreign?
Most if not all of us feel at home with our religions whether foreign or indigenous. No one needs to abandon a religion if you are still attached to it. Continue to attend your foreign church or Mosque or Temple while at the same time reading this book over and over again and discussing the issues with family members and friends. Do not force yourself to abandon a foreign religion when you are not ready. However it is very important to know the facts about your religious beliefs. If you are using a foreign sacred text you may be worshipping a foreign God. You need to decide if it is more important for you to promote the works of your people or the works of foreigners. You also need to decide if you want to go to the heaven of a foreign God or the heaven of the GOD of the Universe. Remember that you are loved without conditions and you are blessed without requirements. And given a choice to choose the WHOLE or one of its parts I encourage you to choose the WHOLE! There is peace, there is understanding, there is tolerance, there is compassion and there is Love! African Spirituality connects you directly to the DIVINE and not to sons and daughters who could send you to hell if you do not believe in them like Jesus.

What should I tell my congregation of Africans worshiping a foreign God?
Continue to do what you have always done until a member of the congregation questions why you continue to worship foreign Gods? Do not answer the question; instead call a meeting of the elders of the church or mosque or temple and discuss the issue. Decide what needs to be done and call a general meeting of the congregation. Give an opportunity to each member to voice their

concerns and what they want done. Whatever you do later will depend on the general consensus of the congregation and your conviction. Meanwhile you may begin to shift the focus of your teachings and sermons from foreign sacred texts to your sacred experiences and the sacred experiences of your people.

I am an African Diaspora; does this message also apply to me?
African Diaspora are Africans who live in other countries and most of you do not have homes in any African country. Obviously your "foreign religion" may not seem "foreign" to you since you were born into it. However in order to understand the importance of an African Spiritual Vision you need to ask yourself the following questions:

1. Who is glorified when you worship a foreign God? It is not the DIVINE but the foreign cultural God and his people. They only give the impression that you are worshiping the DIVINE but in truth you are worshipping a foreign cultural God. To worship the DIVINE you do not need a text that claims to contain the word of God. All you need are your experiences and the experiences of your people because the word of the DIVINE pervades the universe.
2. Who is in control when you minster to a foreign God? If you worship a foreign God you are required to go on pilgrimage to a foreign land. Why not the land in which you were born? Your land is also blessed and there is no need to go on pilgrimage to another land.
3. Whose contributions are proclaimed when you use a foreign sacred text? Did your ancestors contribute anything at all?
4. Who laughs all the way to the bank when you buy a foreign sacred text? Could you use the proceeds from the African Testament of GOD for the education, motivation, economic development and spiritual development of your people?

We may be born into "foreign religions" but as long as we sing the praises of foreigners we are putting aside the contributions of our people for the glorification of foreign Gods and their people. I know how hard it is to fire a foreign cultural God but for the freedom of your people and their well being I encourage you to walk away from all foreign Gods and their texts and never look back as I did! I feel very good and I know you will also feel way better than before. The freedom of your people is more important than going to the heaven of a foreign God and the freedom of your people is also more important even if you would be sent to the hell of a foreign God. But as long as you believe in the DIVINE no foreign God can touch you because a part can never be greater than the WHOLE!!

Can we still keep the teachings of the Foreign Religion after leaving the foreign religion?
This is a very good question because some of us are used to the stories told in our foreign religious texts. I know some of these stories inspired us but we have better stories in real experiences. Our stories are better because we can easily relate to them and learn from them. They are real life stories that inspired many Africans and members of the African Diaspora to fight slavery, apartheid, colonization, segregation, racism and all the evils that we have been subjected to. Walk away from foreign Gods and their sacred texts and do not look back because the DIVINE has better plans for you.

Don't you think we might lose the "protection" from the foreign religion if we leave the foreign religion?
This is another good question in the sense that many people believe that by joining a religion they would be getting some form of mystical or metaphysical "protection" from the religion. I remember some pastors implying that the United States lost the "protection" of God and that was why the terrorists succeeded in destroying the world Trade Center. The idea of protection is the oldest scam in religious history. Many people believe it and I also believed it when I was in High School up to the time I graduated from college.

There was this guy in High School. He was outgoing and seemed very happy with his life. I was the House Captain of my Dormitory and he often disobeyed the school rules. I wondered why he was so happy but did not care about rules? Some said that he belonged to a mystical organization. In my mind I thought if he knew the secret of life at least he should try to be humble.

After High School I looked at my life and I saw no dreams, no hope and no future but I thought if I belonged to this mystical organization I might change my life. Then with the help of friends I joined the organization and started learning. I read their books and practiced meditation for about six months but I did not see the change I wanted. I mean I was able to organize my life but I was still paying bills and sometimes buying things on credit. Organizations give the impression that your life would magically change the moment you join them. This is not the whole truth! However you may learn from the organization and the knowledge could help you to change your life if you applied it but the organization does not have any magical powers to alter your life. In my own case I wouldn't have started meditation without the organization but it did not change my life as I expected. However it is important to know that LIFE is not about miraculously changing your life but about solving problems, overcoming challenges and evolving by applying yourself. If organizations really have mystical powers to change our lives don't you think the world would be different today? But the purpose of life on earth would also be defeated if everything came miraculously!

Look at it this way: if the DIVINE created and blessed all creatures there is no requirement to join an organization. Organizations we join should be such that help us to grow and not how to relate to the DIVINE. Organizations are human creations and they have nothing to do with the blessings of the DIVINE. In some religions you get the "protection" when you accept the presiding God. Supposing you change your mind later and fire the God as I did; does the God remove the "protection"? On the other hand why seek the protection of a cultural God when you already have the blessings of the DIVINE? But is "protection" really that important? If it were so there would be no slavery, no genocide, no colonization, no apartheid, no ethnic cleaning, no holocaust and no any other evil imaginable by the human mind. Finally for the record the DIVINE is not an undeveloped human being that reacts to the environment to remove "protection" when people do not believe and to restore "protection" when they believe! This as I said earlier is a religious scam; do not fall for it!

A foreign God died for my sins, how can I continue to benefit from the sacrifice?
This is a very important question because sin is viewed differently from culture to culture. In some cultures sin is wiped out or washed away with the blood of an animal or a human being. **In African cultures sin is part of the growing up process. No sacrifice is required. Instead the individual learns from his or her sins and becomes a LIGHT to himself and to the people.** Thus in the African spirit you do not need a blood sacrifice; instead believe in the DIVINE, the Divinities and your Ancestors and all will be well with you. Another important thought regarding this question is that if the God is foreign, the God is not your God. **Remember that cultural Gods are only loyal to their people and no amount of accepting a foreign cultural God can change that fact**! Further if you are really concerned about the sacrifice of others for your good have you asked yourself what you have done for others? If you concentrate more on giving to others you may spend less time on taking! Those who concentrate on taking fall for the biggest scams on earth!

Am I required to worship an African God after I leave the foreign religion?
No, no one will be required to worship any God whether foreign or African in the African Spiritual Vision. African religions are mostly family centered and that means that it is your family that decides your religious obligations! Most important is that African religions are founded by Africans and members of the African Diaspora and the message is for the good of all people. Basically this message is "You are loved without conditions and you are blessed without requirements". In a typical family religious assembly the DIVINE is at the center followed by the family's favorite Divinities and the ancestors. During individual meditation family members may get in tune with the Divine, worship your favorite Divinities and the Ancestors. The choice is up to you.

I was born in Africa but my ancestors are from outside Africa, how does this message affect me?

Your ancestors may come from a different continent but as long as you were born in Africa, you are also an African. However it is your choice to practice an African religion or the religion of your ancestors in your family. Spirituality is a personal journey and the attitude is for each person to draw from all spiritual traditions that make sense to the individual. When I had the hole in my heart I read many spiritual and circular books but it was a book from India, the Upanishads, that sealed the hole. Does that mean I should convert to Hinduism? My answer is "No". I appreciate the contribution of the book during my moments of uncertainty but that does not mean that I should automatically be a Hindu. The journey is still mine and I make the choices. In the same way the journey is still yours and you make the choices! That you live in the continent of Africa does not mean that you should automatically convert to an African religion.

In the main African religions are not organized religions and there is no need for conversion, no need to promise heaven and no need to threaten hell! African religions are family religions that stem from the DIVINE and it is up to each family to interpret the DIVINE message for the well being of the family. However, this is an opportunity for unity in the continent and I encourage you to join your fellow Africans to write the African Testament of GOD.

THE DIRECT LINE

Some cultures teach that because of our sins we cannot connect directly with the DIVINE but we could do so with the help of a mediator. Other cultures teach that we are already connected to the DIVINE and that sin is part of the developing process of the individual and it does not prevent anyone from connecting with the DIVINE. You can see that we have different teachings from different cultures but that is alright because we see the DIVINE differently. However we should be careful and use our personal experiences and wisdom to choose what is right for us and not to believe a culture blindly even if it is your culture. There is always room for improvement.

The Direct Line Argument helps us to examine the two positions: can we connect with the DIVINE directly or do we really need a mediator? I will illustrate this dichotomy with the help of the telephone as we knew it before the computer revolution. Let us assume that Abu has a telephone and he always made a connection each time he dialed. Now suppose that he stumbled upon a book about telephones that was written over 2,000 years ago. Abu's first reaction was 'what could our 2,000 year old ancestors know about telephones?' But he read the book with an open mind and found out to his surprise that there were some facts about telephones that are consistent with modern thinking. There were however, a few ideas that were not true based on our current knowledge. One in particular said that no one could make a connection without an operator. Now let us assume that Abu also has some knowledge about telephones and he has made many direct connections without operator's assistance in the past. His first reaction after reading this claim was 'how ignorant our ancestors were' and went about his business.

Kwame on the other hand has also made some direct connections in the past but lately he has not been able to make any connection. However like Abu he also stumbled upon the book on telephones and read the same information. But unlike Abu, Kwame does not know anything about telephones so he believed the book that he could not make a direct connection without operator's assistance. Meanwhile Kwane began to doubt the connections he made in the past and seemed helpless and confused. As he sat in his apartment thinking of how he could get an operator's assistance he heard a knock. Kwame opened the door and behold there was a telephone connection service person restoring connections in the neighborhood for a fee. Kwame paid the fee and his telephone service was restored.

Direct Line Interpretation
The book in the story represents a cultural sacred text. The connection is the DIVINE. We are all connected to the DIVINE and Abu knew this truth and has always been connected to the DIVINE. Abu maintains his connection even when he has problems. He doesn't need a mediator. Kwame on the other hand does not know much about the DIVINE so the moment he got into problems he started to look outside for help. He believed the book that he does not have direct access to the DIVINE and that cost him not only money but also peace of mind. Beware of the things you read from foreign sacred texts because they could complicate your life!

Who are you?
Are you a Moslem? Are you a European? Are you a Chinese? Are you Black? Are you a Minister? Some of these "labels" may apply to you but what is your natural essence? Society has put "labels"

on all of us to overshadow our true identity in order to manipulate, divide, discriminate, enslave, abuse, control, deceive, instigate and so on. In order to truly know who you are you need to remove all the "labels". Just for a moment forget that you are a Moslem, European, Chinese, Black or a Minister. If you are in your bedroom or somewhere private go ahead and remove what you are wearing and look at yourself in the mirror from head to your feet. What you see is what every man is if you are a man and it is what every woman is if you are a woman. Remember this image each time you think that you are a Moslem, European, Chinese, Black or a Minister. LIFE treats us the same way and the health of the human race depends on identifying with the whole rather than with a unit!

Beyond this image of oneness is also a unique individual with talents to cultivate and gifts to share with the rest of the world. If you really need an operator she must be one to remind you that you live in a world driven by LOVE and the fact that you live in it means that you are blessed! You are a creature of hope, dreams, accomplishments, prosperity, health, love, faith, understanding, progress, expression, vitality, reason, communication, perception, appreciation and all other spiritual realities stemming from the DIVINE. You can test this truth by observing a child. Any normal child is usually happy, independent, confident, curious, fearless, loving, sensitive, empathetic, hopeful, and gets all she needs or wants. She is not a loser and she is certainly not fallen! Instead she is a co-creator and that is who you are!

FAMOUS SACRED TEXTS

Sacred texts are religious texts regarded as inspired by believers. Moslems believe that Allah dictated the Koran to Mohammad. There is a story that the Prophet meditated daily in the forest and one day a voice said, "Write". And that was how the Koran came to be. Jews believe that God gave the Torah to Moses. Christians believe that the Bible is the inspired word of God and that it is infallible and inerrant. Inerrant means that it has no errors. Hindus believe that the Vedas were directly received by sages from God and passed on to generations by word of mouth before they were written down. And of course Buddhists, Jains, Sikhs and other religions also believe that their religious books were inspired. If you are reading this and thinking that one of all these texts must be the truly inspired text your thought is faulty because in the affairs of the DIVINE we are all one. The DIVINE does not discriminate as the cultural Gods. Further the DIVINE is everywhere and anyone could tap into the DIVINE.

There are no chosen people and no nation is set apart to do the work of the DIVINE. Above all there are no sacred texts for the DIVINE. The Universe is the only sacred text for the DIVINE. It is open to all people to observe and interpret. At best our Sacred Texts are sacred experiences from different cultural perspectives. They are not the words of the DIVINE; instead they are the words of men and there is a great difference between the words of the DIVINE and the words of men. The African Testament of GOD is a human document that highlights our experiences in the world and with the sacred; it is not the word of the DIVINE! No human text can contain the word of the DIVINE!

Cultural Gods are products of a culture because it is their experience. In this sense you cannot take one cultural God to another culture and tell the people that you have brought God to them. You may have taken your God to them but you did not take the DIVINE to them. The DIVINE is everywhere and cannot be taken to any culture. You could take your experience of the DIVINE to a people but that is very wrong because it is not their experience and it is useless to them. Would you prefer to tell a foreign story to your children or the stories of your culture? That is precisely the point. The practice of exporting our sacred experiences enslaves the mind. It is useless to the people, it is unacceptable and it goes against all the tenets of freedom!

However if you strongly believe that your text is the only true text it is naïve to think that others do not feel strongly about their own texts. Perhaps knowing that others are also like us is the first step toward acceptance and understanding. We can no longer ignore or deny the contributions of other cultures. It is not enough to tolerate other religions because like us they have erected breathtaking buildings to their cultural Gods or to the DIVINE. Like us they share their sacred experiences with their children and with the world. However there are still many cultures that are waiting for the time to write their sacred experiences for the benefit of their children and the world. I hope this book will give you the green light to begin. The world is waiting anxiously for your sacred experiences!

I have already stated that religious books are products of culture. They were not written for all people. Instead they are the experiences of cultures. Thus if you are an African and you picked up a copy of the Bhagavad Gita, for instance and begin to read, in fact before you even open to the first page the title will automatically tell you that you are about to read a book from another culture. The title of the New Testament does not readily show it as a foreign text if you speak English but as soon as you begin to read it you will sooner or later grasp its foreign origin, that is, from the point of view of an African. We know where these texts originated and their contents in most cases promote their cultural heritage and that is why they are not universal texts but I must confess that the Buddhist Sutras, the Upanishads, the Tao Te

Ching and the Bhagavad Gita come close to being universal sacred texts.

I know we have promoted our sacred texts as universal documents and the unsuspecting natives now embrace many foreign texts as their own. But one must be really ignorant to believe that a foreign text is for their good. This is not to imply that there is nothing good in the foreign texts. In fact many of them including the New Testament have universal teachings that could be applied in other cultures. The point is that no foreign text should dominate another culture. The foreign text must always occupy a subordinate position if it is at all used in another culture. But the product of the culture should always stand supreme however inferior it is.

Don't you feel small when you open a foreign sacred text to read about the stories of their ancestors? Who reads about the stories of your ancestors? Don't you feel enslaved again when your whole life depends on foreign religious beliefs? Did your ancestors not learn anything about life? Don't you feel colonized again when you use foreign religious texts in your national ceremonies? Are you really a sovereign nation? Don't you feel guilty each time you open a foreign sacred text to read about their accomplishments? Did you accomplish anything at all?

No people on earth have experienced what you have experienced but why did you not write these experiences in sacred literature for your children? Do you believe that your experiences do not count toward the general good? But on a closer examination you are not to be totally blamed for the state of things. The colonizers and slave masters spread their religion at the time you were most vulnerable. Anyone could sell anything to a slave and a colonized nation! If a foreign religion gained popularity because of slavery and colonization I do not think it is a real victory. They used their position to take advantage of unsuspecting people. The good news is that what humans have put together can always be dismantled.

The better news is that the DIVINE has heard the prayers of the enslaved, the colonized and all the nations that were mistreated in the past. It is now their turn to be king!

Hindu Sacred Texts

The Hindu sacred literature is divided into two distinct categories: Sruti or Shruti and Smriti. Shruti represent the texts that are "heard", meaning that they were divinely revealed. Spiritual truths were revealed to sages or rishis who transmitted them to the people in the form of oral tradition before they were written down. The revealed texts consist of the Samhitas, the Brahmanas, the Aranyakas and the Upanishads. Smriti on the other hand represent the texts that are "remembered", meaning that they were passed down by humans but are based on the revealed truths. In other words Smriti are texts based on human understanding and effort and these texts include the Epics, the Sutras and the Puranas. An epic is a long poem that narrates the conquests of a hero. The famous epics are the Mahabarata and the Ramyana. The Mahabarata includes the Bhagavad Gita. Lord Krishna is the hero in the Mahabarata (the Bhagavad Gita) and Lord Rama is the hero in the Ramayana. A Sutra is a collection of teachings about life. The Suras are a collection of texts dealing with Dharma, Yoga and Vedanta. One of the famous sutras is the Laws of Manu. The Puranas are a collection of texts on mythology, rituals, hymns, history and rules of life. The most famous puranas are Vishnu Purana, Bhagavata Purana and Shiva Purana.

Quotes About the Vedas
The Vedas especially, the Upanishads, came to my rescue and changed my view of the DIVINE during my religious crisis. My research shows that I am not the only person who has benefited

from this sacred knowledge and I believe anyone who gets a taste of the teachings of these sacred texts will equally be transformed.

Arthur Schopenhauer was a German Philosopher regarded as one of the greatest philosophers of the 19th century. His thoughts on the Vedas and the Upanishads are contagious: *The "Vedas are the most rewarding and the most elevating book which can be possible in the world."* Schopenhauer, also wrote in *The World as Will and Idea* that the *Upanishads were the most beneficial and elevating study that the world had ever produced and that 'it has been the solace of my life, it will be the solace of my death'*

Aldous Huxley was an English writer best known for his work on the Brave New World and the Perennial Philosophy. Here are his thoughts on the Bhagavad Gita: *The Bhagavad-Gita is the most systematic statement of spiritual evolution of endowing value to mankind. It is one of the most clear and comprehensive summaries of perennial philosophy ever revealed; hence its enduring value is subject not only to India but to all of humanity."*

Pandit Jawaharlal Nehru was a humanist and became the first prime minister of India after India gained her independence from Britain. His thoughts on the Bhagavad Gita are worthy of note: *The Bhagavad-Gita deals essentially with the spiritual foundation of human existence. It is a call of action to meet the obligations and duties of life; yet keeping in view the spiritual nature and grander purpose of the universe."*

William James was an American Psychologist and philosopher. He is popularly known for his essay on "the one and the many". Here are his thoughts on the Vedas: *From the Vedas we learn a practical art of surgery, medicine, music, house building under which mechanized art is included. They are encyclopedia of every aspect of life, culture, religion, science, ethics, law, cosmology and meteorology.*

Mahatma Ghandi was a Hindu and a great Indian leader who taught us the importance of ahimsa, the doctrine of non-violence. His quote on the Bhagavad Gita is revealing: *The Gita is the universal mother. I find a solace in the Bhagavad Gita that I miss even in the Sermon on the Mount. When disappointment stares me in the face and all alone I see not one ray of light, I go back to the Bhagavad Gita. I find a verse here and a verse there, and I immediately begin to smile in the midst of overwhelming tragedies - and my life has been full of external tragedies - and if they have left no visible or indelible scar on me, I owe it all to the teaching of Bhagavad Gita."*

Henry David Thoreau was an American author, poet and philosopher. He is remembered for his book "Waden", a reflection upon simple living in natural surroundings, and his essay "Resistance to Civil Government", an argument for disobedience to an unjust state. His thoughts on the Vedas are uniting: *Whenever I have read any part of the Vedas, I have felt that some unearthly and unknown light illuminated me. In the great teaching of the Vedas, there is no touch of the sectarianism. It is of ages, climes, and nationalities and is the royal road for the attainment of the Great Knowledge. When I am at it, I feel that I am under the spangled heavens of a summer night.*

Max Muller was a German scholar who translated many eastern sacred texts including the Upanishads. Here are his thoughts on Hindu Spiritual Literature: *If I were to look over the whole world to find out the country most richly endowed with all the wealth, power and beauty that nature can bestow — in some parts a very paradise on earth — I should point to India. If I were asked under what sky the human mind has most fully developed the choicest gifts, has most deeply pondered on the greatest problems of life, and has found solution of some of them which well deserve the attention even of those who have studied Plato and Kant-I should point to India. And if I were to ask myself from what literature we here in Europe, we who have been nurtured almost exclusively on the thought of Greeks and Romans, and of one Semitic race, the Jewish, may draw that corrective which is most wanted in order to make our inner life more perfect, more comprehensive, more universal, in fact more truly human, a life not for this life only, but a transfigured and eternal life-again I should point to India.*

Famous Vedic Teachings

Without doubt the Bhagavad Gita has illuminated many minds on our planet. Some call it "a call to action" others see in it as containing the stuff that would lead each of us to our desired goals and it does that without infringing on our beliefs or compromising our temperaments. You can choose the path of faith, the path of devotion, the path of meditation, the path of work or your own path and you can find perennial spiritual teachings to lead you to your destination. Thus the famous or most important teaching of the Bhagavad Gita is its message of inclusion and freedom of choice. When Arjuna asked Lord Krishna what he should do to attain the supreme the Savior did not just present him with a single path but many and that the choice was his. This freedom of choice regarding our spiritual aspirations is one of the most important Vedic teachings. In a worldly sense the Bhagavad Gita seems to be a book about war but spiritually this war is not anywhere else but within us! Personally the most important Vedic spiritual literature are the Upanishads. They are important to me because they came to my rescue in my moments of doubt. They restored my love for the DIVINE not from another culture's perspective but from my own experiences and the experiences of my people!

Christian Sacred Texts

The Bible is the major sacred text in Christianity. The Bible simply means books. Christians believe that the Bible is the word of God and it is infallible and inerrant.

The Bible contains two testaments: the Old and the New Testaments. A testament is a will but in the case of the Bible it is a covenant between God and people. The Old Testament is a testament between God and the people of Israel. The New Testament is a testament between God and the Church. The Protestant Old Testament is identical to the Jewish Tanakh and it is made up of 39 books including Genesis, Exodus, Leviticus, Numbers, Deuteronomy, Joshua, Judges, Ruth, 1 Samuel, 2 Samuel, 1 Kings, 2 Kings, 1 Chronicles, 2 Chronicles, Ezra, Nehemiah, Esther, Job, Psalms, Proverbs, Ecclesiastes, Song of Songs, Isaiah, Jeremiah, Lamentations, Ezekiel, Daniel, Hosea, Joel, Amos, Obadiah, Jonah, Micah, Nahum, Habakkuk, Zephaniah, Haggai, Zechariah, and Malachi.

The Catholic Old Testament has 46 books and is made up of Genesis, Exodus, Leviticus, Numbers, Deuteronomy, Joshua, Judges, Ruth, 1 Samuel, 2 Samuel, 1 Kings, 2 Kings, 1 Chronicles, 2 Chronicles, Ezra, Nehemiah, Tobit, Judith, Esther, 1 Maccabees, 2 Maccabees, Job, Psalms, Proverbs, Ecclesiastes, Song of Songs, Wisdom, Sirach, Isaiah, Jeremiah, Lamentations, Baruch, Ezekiel, Daniel, Hosea, Joel, Amos, Obadiah, Jonah, Micah, Nahum, Habakkuk, Zephaniah, Haggai, Zechariah, and Malachi. The New Testament contains 27 books including Matthew, Mark, Luke, John, Acts of the Apostles, Romans, 1 Corinthians, 2 Corinthians, Galatians, Ephesians, Philippians, Colossians, 1 Thessalonians, 2 Thessalonians, 1 Timothy, 2 Timothy, Titus, Philemon, Hebrews, James, 1 Peter, 2 Peter, 1 John, 2 John, 3 John, Jude and Revelation.

Quotes about the Bible
Like the Vedas there are also many people who have found fulfillment with the Bible. It was the first sacred text I knew and I enjoyed the Psalms, Proverbs and Ecclesiastes. I also recall an incident in which my Bible was the source of favor from Biafran soldiers. During the Nigerian – Biafran War I violated a Biafran Law. It was against the law to have any Nigerian money at the time. When Nigerian money was still in use in Biafra my Dad gave me some money and I put the paper money in my math book. As time passed I forgot about the money because I had no need for the

money. My uncle was taking good care of me. One day Biafran soldiers came to our small town searching for Nigerian soldiers that might be hiding in our homes. Their searches were very thorough because they looked into every nook and corner including between pages in books and they found the paper money my Dad gave to me a while back.

As I recall three of us were guilty of this crime. Violations of this kind usually got one to be killed by a firing squad but because of the town's cooperation with the Biafran Government we were given a lighter sentence--whipping. They took us to the center of the town and whipped us till blood started gushing out from our backs. For me I thought it was the end so I stayed motionless but one of the officers thought I might be dead and asked the officer who was whipping me to stop. Then the officer who was concerned about my life came and kicked me to make sure I was still alive. I regained consciousness and got up and the officer who was whipping me said something like "If you think the Nigerians are coming back you should think again because Biafra is here to stay".

 To say the least that was my first taste of hell on earth. It took me many months to heal. After healing I decided to leave the town to the plantation where I grew up when I lived with my grandmother. I thought I would be safe in the plantation without Biafran soldiers watching my every move. So I planned and left for the Plantation with my aunt and another relative. I had my Bible with me. On the way we were stopped by Biafran soldiers for a routine check. The soldiers I was trying to avoid where everywhere. They went through all our belongings including my Bible. One of them picked up the Bible and started checking the pages. In reaction I thought "if you are looking for another Nigerian money, you are too late." But as he opened the pages of the Bible his face lightened up. He saw the address of the High School I attended before the war and asked if I knew him. I told him that his face looked familiar but I did not know where to place him. Then he told me that he was one of the brothers of the proprietor of the school I attended. With that said he let us go without any more questions. Here are some of the quotes about the Bible:

Mahatma Gandhi was influenced by several religions including Christianity. Here are his thoughts on the New Testament: *"The New Testament gave me comfort and boundless joy, as it came after the revulsion that parts of the Old Testament had given me. Today, supposing I was deprived of the Gita and forgot all its contents but had a copy of the Sermon on the Mount, I should derive the same joy from it as I do from the Gita".*

Charles Dickens was an English writer and was popularly known for his works on A Tale of Two Cities, Oliver Twist, and Great Expectations. Here are his thoughts on the New Testament: *The New Testament is the very best book that ever was or ever will be known in the world.*

William Jennings Bryan was the 41st United States Secretary of State under President Woodrow Wilson. His quote about the Bible stems from his beliefs. *"The BIBLE holds up before us ideals that are within sight of the weakest and the lowliest, and yet so high that the best and the noblest are kept with their faces turned ever upward. It carries the call of the Savior to the remotest corners of the earth; on its pages are written the assurances of the present and our hopes for the future"*

Samuel Taylor Coleridge was an English poet, literary critic and philosopher. He is well known for the "Rime of the Ancient Mariner". Hs quote about the Bible is worthy of note: *"For more than a thousand years the BIBLE, collectively taken, has gone hand in hand with civilization, science, law -- in short, with the moral and intellectual cultivation of the species, always supporting and often leading the way"*

Famous Biblical Teachings
The Sermon on the Mount is one of the famous spiritual teachings of the New Testament. Among others the Sermon on the Mount teaches us to love our enemies, give to the needy, pray in secret, fast and build treasures in heaven. Regarding the circumstances of our lives the sermon teaches us not to worry about anything because God knows about the demands of our lives; instead all we

need to do is to ask and we will receive, seek and we will find, knock and the door will be open for us. These teachings are life changing and the good news is that you don't have to be a Christian to benefit from them.

They are universal teachings that would enrich your life for generations after generations. However my most important biblical teaching is the Parable of the Good Samaritan. The parable is so important to me because it was one of the first stories I learned in Grade School. Our teacher did not only tell the story he also put it in the form of a song. Apparently our teacher, Mr. Ezenwa, knew how to capture a child's imagination and that song was one of my favorite songs. I sang it for my family and for others who cared to listen. The Parable of the Good Samaritan is a parable about compassion and taking care of each other irrespective of our color, race, religion or nationality. Here is my version of the parable of the Good Samaritan:

Once upon a time a lawyer went to Jesus in order to test him. The lawyer asked what he should do to inherit eternal life. Jesus asked him about what was written in the law regarding these matters and the lawyer answered that he should love God with all his heart and with all his soul and with all his strength and with all his mind and that he should also love his neighbor as himself. Jesus congratulated him on his answer and advised him to live by what he has just said and he would live. But the lawyer wanted to demonstrate his learning and asked Jesus who his neighbor was? In reply Jesus shared the Parable of the Good Samaritan.

A man was traveling from Jerusalem to Jericho and was attacked by highway robbers. They took his belonging including his clothes and beat him mercilessly and left him half dead by the side of the road. After the incident a priest passed by the same road but on seeing the half dead man by the way side he decided to take another road. A Levite also took the same road but on seeing the man he too took another road. Then a Samaritan also came by the same road. He was moved by pity and compassion when he saw the helpless man by the roadside. Immediately the Samaritan went to the victim and treated his wounds. Next he took the man to an inn and took care of him. The next day he entrusted the man with the innkeeper and paid for all his expenses but also assured the innkeeper that he would return after his travels and reimburse him for any extra expenses on behalf of the man. New Testament: Luke 10:25-37

Buddhist Sacred Texts

Buddhist Sacred Texts are not revealed truths from a God, instead they are guides from the Buddha on the path of truth. The main Buddhist Sacred Text is the Tipitaka or Tripitaka, also called the Pali Canon since it was written in Pali. Tripitika simply means three Baskets, thus the text has three sections including a Sutta Pitaka, containing the Buddha's Discourses; a Vinaya Pitaka, containing the monastic Code; and an Abhidhamma Pitaka containing the philosophical commentaries on the Buddha's teachings. The other important sacred texts include the Mahayana Sutras, the Tibetan Buddhist Canon and the Jataka Tales.

Quotes about Buddhism

Albert Einstein was a physicist and was popularly known for his theory of relativity but his quote on Buddhism is revealing and I quote: *"Buddhism has the characteristics of what would be expected in a cosmic religion for the future: It transcends a personal God, avoids dogmas and theology; it covers both the natural and spiritual; and it is based on a religious sense aspiring from the experience of all things, natural and spiritual, as a meaningful unity. If there is any religion that would cope with modern scientific needs it would be Buddhism. "On the religion of the future Albert Einstein said "The religion of the future will be a cosmic religion. The religion which based on experience, which refuses dogmatic. If there's any religion that would cope the scientific needs it will be Buddhism"*

Bhimrao Ramji Ambedkar was an Indian scholar, nationalist, jurist, political leader, Buddhist revivalist and an architect of the Indian Constitution. His quote on Buddhism is enlightening: *"I prefer Buddhism because it gives three principles in combination, which no other religion does. Buddhism teaches prajna (understanding as against superstition and supernaturalism), karuna (love), and samata (equality). This is what man wants for a good and happy life. Neither god nor soul can save society.*

Herbie Hancock is an American pianist and composer. Here are his thoughts on Buddhism: *Buddhism opened me up to seeing things from the standpoint of being a human being- looking at the purpose of action and the effects on life.*

Bertrand Russell was a British philosopher, logician, mathematician, historian, advocate for social reform, and pacifist. His quote on Buddhism spells the nature of the religion: *Of the great religions of history I prefer Buddhism, especially in its earliest forms because it has had the smallest element of persecution.*

Richard Dawkins is an English Ethologist, Evolutionary Biologist and author. He is popularly known for his books the Selfish Gene, the Blind Watchmaker and the God Delusion. His thoughts on Buddhism and Hinduism are enlightening: *Hinduism and Buddhism offer much more sophisticated worldviews (or philosophies) and I see nothing wrong with these religions.*

Dr Carl Jung was a Swiss psychologist/psychiatrist and Founder of the Jungian school of psychology. Here is his thought on Buddhism: *As a student of comparative religion, I believe that Buddhism is the most perfect one the world has even seen. The*

91

philosophy of the theory of evolution and the law of karma were far superior to any other creed. It was neither the history of religion nor the study of philosophy that first drew me to the world of Buddhist thought but my professional interest as a doctor. My task was to treat psychic suffering and it was this that impelled me to become acquainted with the views and methods of that great teacher of humanity, whose principal theme was the chain of suffering, old age, sickness and death.

Famous Buddhist Teachings

Without hesitation I humbly join the above-mentioned luminaries to declare Buddhism as the greatest religion and the religion of the future in the sense that anyone who wants to develop himself or herself could learn from buddhism. It seems like every step you take in Buddhism takes you closer to your ultimate goal-your goal for living. What is your purpose in life? What do you want to contribute? What do you want to have? What do you want to share? You decide and it will be done! It will be done because this is your life and you are in control! Buddhism gives you the resources to pierce the veil of illusion so that you may see life for what it really is. In short it is your ball.

Now should I begin with the Four Noble Truths that proclaim the nature of life on earth or with the Noble Eightfold Path that teaches us how to live on earth? Do not forget the Jataka Tales that teach us how to live a virtuous life? How about the Lotus Sutra that teaches us that all beings may reach Buddhahood and attain Nirvana? This in a way is similar to the Unitarian Universalist Affirmation that no one is saved until we are all saved. These teachings give us a sense that we are not alone and what other better way is there to live this life than to live it taking care of each other?

What strikes me most when I think about Buddhism is the Buddha himself. I believe he is the greatest man that ever lived on earth! I cannot get over anyone who abandons a privileged life in order to dedicate his or her life to serve humanity. It is unbelievable but that was exactly what the Buddha did! Now for my favorite Buddhist teachings, there are many but the Parable of the Burning House and the Parable of the Poison Arrow stand supreme.

In the Parable of the Burning House a rich man and his children lived in a large house. One day the house caught fire when the children were playing. Like any parent the father was quick to tell the children that the house was burning and that they should all get out immediately. Meanwhile the children have not seen the fire and they were so absorbed in their play that they ignored his pleas to get out of the building. Then he decided to promise them something they could not refuse. He told them that waiting for them outside were three kinds of carts that they have always wanted: a cart pulled by a goat, another by a deer and a third by an Ox. On hearing about the gifts the children immediately ran out of the building to get their carts. The father was relieved and thanked the children for getting out of the house but confessed that he really does not have three carts but only one cart that is superior to all the three carts put together. He gave the children the magnificent cart and advised them to play with the cart together.

The Parable of the Burning House is told in the Lotus sutra with more details than I have presented here but what stands out for me is the idea of using skillful means in life and the story reminds me of a Kenyan Doctor who was spat on by a White Supremacist during an emergency call. I also shared the story with our 8-year old son and asked if the father told a lie? According to our son, the father did not tell a lie because no one asked him to tell the truth instead he made up a story in order to get the children out of the burning house! What was important was getting the children out but he did not stop there he also gave them a better cart than the individual carts he promised. Things change in life!

My other important Buddhist parable is the Parable of the Poison Arrow and it concerned the Buddha and one of his disciples, *Malunkyaputta.* Most if not all of us sometimes doubt our beliefs and teachings from our teachers. If we are brave enough we could confront those beliefs and teachings by doing research and if it is from our teacher we could share our points of conflict with the teacher. Malunkyaputta was having one of those moments of doubt and had lots of questions to ask the Buddha. He was concerned that the Buddha had left many things unexplained and wanted to know if the world is eternal? He wanted to know if the soul is different from the body and if there is life after death? He was so concerned about the answers to these questions that he resolved to return to worldly life if the Buddha did not give him a satisfactory answer.

One day the Buddha was sitting with his disciples and *Malunkyaputta approched him with his questions. In response the Buddha asked Malunkyaputta to imagine that he were wounded by a poisonous arrow shot from a distance and his family took him to a surgeon to remove the arrow. Now suppose that he refused treatment because he wanted to know the name of the man who shot the arrow, the nature of the bow, and the nature of the arrow that wounded him. Some people may want to find out about such things but meanwhile the poison will slowly attack his vital organs and he will die before anyone could find out about the person who shot the arrow, the nature of the bow and the nature of the arrow. In the same way if anyone decides not to live a noble life under the Buddha until the Buddha answers metaphysical questions, the person will die. The fact is that whether we believe in an afterlife or not there is still birth, old age, death, grief, suffering, sorrow and despair. But all these can be destroyed in this life if we heed to the teachings.*

According to the Buddha he has not explained metaphysical issues because they are not useful and they are not conducive to tranquility and Nirvana. What he has explained is suffering, the cause of suffering, the destruction of suffering and the path that leads to the destruction of suffering. *"This is useful because it leads to non-attachment, the absence of passion and perfect knowledge. The Buddha spoke thus to Malunkyaputta and with joy Malunkyaputta applauded the Buddha's teachings.*

Sacred Texts of Islam

There are two main sacred texts in Islam. They include the Qur'an (or Koran) and the Hadith (or Hadeeth). Moslems believe that the Qur'an is the direct word of Allah as revealed by the angel Gabriel to Muhammad. Allah is an Arabic word for God. The Hadith on the other hand contains sayings and deeds of Muhammad and his followers. The Qur'an contains 114 chapters or Suras of varying lengths. Each chapter is made up of several verses known as ayat. There are 6236 verses in the Qur'an.

Quotes about the Qur'an

The Qur'an has often been denounced by people who did not know anything about it. This closeness of mind is what results in all the atrocities we have committed in the past against our fellow human beings. We believe that our book is the true and only sacred text and with that notion we discriminate and sometimes even kill people who do not believe like us. Here are some quotes about the Qur'an.

Karen Armstrong is a British author and commentator popularly known for her books on religion. Her thoughts on Islam is enlightening: *"It is as though Muhammad had created an entirely new literary form that some people were not ready for but which thrilled others. Without this experience of the Koran, it is extremely unlikely that Islam would have taken root. We have seen that it took the ancient Israelites some seven hundred years to break with their old religious allegiances and accept monotheism but Muhammad managed to help the Arabs achieve this difficult transition in a mere twenty-three years. Muhammad as poet and prophet and the Koran as text and theophany is surely an unusually striking instance of the deep congruence that exists between art and religion."*

Professor Keith Moore of the University of Toronto is a professor emeritus. His thoughts on the Qur'an are revealing: *"It has been a great pleasure for me to help clarify statements in the Qur'an about human development. It is clear to me that these statements must have come to Muhammad from God, or 'Allah', because almost all of this knowledge was not discovered until many centuries later. This proves to me that Muhammad must have been a messenger of Allah"*

Dr Steingass. *"The Koran admittedly occupies an important position among the great religious books of the world. Though the youngest of the epoch making works belonging to this class of literature, it yields to hardly any in the wonderful effect which it has produced on large masses of men. It has created an all but new phase of human thought and a fresh type of character. It first transformed a number of heterogeneous desert tribes of the Arabian peninsula into a nation of heroes, and then proceeded to create the vast politico-religious organizations of Mohammedan world which are one of the great forces with which Europe and the East have to reckon today."*

Rev. G. Margoliouth. *"The essential and definite element of my conversion to Islam was the Qur'an. I began to study it before my conversion with the critical spirit of a Western intellectual .... There are certain verses of this book, the Qur'an, revealed more than thirteen centuries ago, which teach exactly the same notions as the most modern scientific researches do. This definitely converted me."*

Ali Selman Benoist, France, Doctor of Medicine. *"I have read the Sacred Scriptures of every religion; nowhere have I found what I encountered in Islam: perfection. The Holy Qur'an, compared to any other scripture I have read, is like the Sun compared to that of a match. I firmly believe that anybody who reads the Word of Allah with a mind that is not completely closed to Truth, will become a Muslim."* **Saifuddin Dirk** Walter Mosig

Famous Teachings of the Qur'an

The most famous teaching of the Qur'an is Tawhid or the Oneness of God. This belief is so central in the Qur'an that the first Sura begins with the affirmation that there is only one God:

"You alone we worship. You alone we ask for help". (Sura 1:5).

In this sense Islam is a truly monotheistic religion and separates itself from some of the other world religions that have other Gods or Saviours who act as intermediaries.

My favourite teaching from the Qur'an concerns the sacrifice by Abraham. If you read the Tanakh you probably learned that Abraham attempted to sacrifice his son Isaac but in the Qur'an it sounds like Ishmael but did not outright mention it. The two stories present an interesting religious understanding. How could two religions that claim to worship the same God make such contradictory statements about their God? What effect does this contradiction have on believers and non-believers?

It has been suggested that the contradiction does not seem to bother any of the groups because each group thinks that the other is wrong. But for an outsider like myself in search of the religion of my people the contradiction matters.

Two thoughts immediately come to mind: Doubt and Revelation. There is doubt in the sense that I do not know which text to believe. I know the Tanakh came before the Qur'an but hearing from both sides is more informative than hearing from only one side. However this information does not solve the problem about who is right and who is wrong. Personally I do not think that it is even a question of who is right and who is wrong. Instead the two texts teach us about the diversity in human narratives.

When I go past "who is right and who is wrong" I come face to face with revelation. What are these two texts telling me? They are telling me that God cannot be pinned down. The fact that contradictory views exist side by side means that no one really has the last say on GOD. We may have books that we consider to be the "word of GOD", but that is just one view out of millions, billions and trillions of views. In other words the images of God we have in our sacred texts and in our temples do not really define the DIVINE. The DIVINE is nameless and stands above human categories. Hence the DIVINE can only be in our thoughts and if we decide to personalize the DIVINE we will be part of millions and billions and trillions of other images. **That is why it is wrong to preach your image of God in another culture. It limits the limitlessness of GOD and robs the natives of their own experiences.**

According to the Tanakh Sarai, Abraham's wife had a servant from Egypt called Hagar. At the time Sarai had no children so she decided to give Hagar to Abraham as his wife. Her motive was to build a family through her handmaid and Hagar gave birth to Ishmael. It seems from this brief genealogy that we have a family relationship between the Jews and the Arabs. If we do why should a foreigner or an outsider choose between them? The significance of this story is to encourage other cultures to write their own sacred texts and share with the world

Never again will natives approach the DIVINE through the experiences of other cultures. Never again will cultures bow down to foreign Gods. Never again will other nations use foreign texts. The practice is against all principles of freedom and it is inconsistent with Universal Love. From this day henceforth natives will write their own sacred texts and live according to their experiences. They will replace all foreign sacred texts with their own sacred texts and all foreign Gods with their own Gods and put an end to the slavery of the mind. This is the Universal Spiritual Vision! And it is done!

Taoist Sacred Texts

The major sacred texts are the Tao Te Ching and Chuang-tzu. Other Taoist Sacred Texts include the *Lieh-tzu, Ling pao Ching and the T'ai-p'ing Ching.* The Tao Te Ching (or Dao de Jing), is a collection of 81 poems and stories written by Lao Tzu around the sixth century B.C.E. Lao Tzu was an older contemporary of Confucius. Writing the Tao Te Ching was not a focus of his life; he only wrote it after much persuasion from his followers. Understandably no one can write about the DIVINE because the DIVINE is unknown. We can only write about our cultural Gods and our cultural Gods have nothing to do with the rest of the world. But the Tao Te Ching has a lot to offer to the rest of the world because it does not dwell on cultural and ethnic Gods. The Tao Te Ching deals with the mystery of the universe and Lao Tzu's style cuts across cultures in his narration. It is a book about life and how to live it with understanding and faith. Get your copy today.

The author, Chuang Tzu or Zhuang Zi ,of Chuang Tzu lived around 369-298 B.C.E. The book was written around the 14th century B.C.E. and it consists of stories, tales and jokes about life.

Quotes about the Tao Te Ching
The Tao Te Ching is one of the most popular sacred texts in the world. It is small but its teachings can cover a whole life of contemplation. Here are some famous quotes about the Tao Te Ching:

Robert Friedler. The *Tao Te Ching has served as a personal road map for millions of people. It is said that its words reveal the underlying principles that govern the world in which we live. Holding to the laws of nature, drawing from the essence of what all things are, it offers both a moral compass and an internal balance.*

Gia-Fu Feng & Jane English: *A fundamental book of the Taoist, the Tao Te Ching is regarded as a revelation in its own right. For those seeking a better understanding of themselves, it provides a wealth of wisdom and insights.*

Stephen Mitchell: *Lao-tzu's Tao Te Ching, or Book of the Way, is the classic manual on the art of living, and one of the wonders of the world. In eighty-one brief chapters, the Tao Te Ching looks at the basic predicament of being alive and gives advice that imparts balance and perspective, a serene and generous spirit. This book is about wisdom in action. It teaches how to work for the good with the effortless skill that comes from being in accord with the Tao (the basic principle of the universe) and applies equally to good government and sexual love; to child rearing, business, and ecology.*

Famous Tao Te Ching Teachings

One of the most famous teachings of the Tao Te Ching begins with what the Tao is not.

"The Tao that can be told is not the eternal Tao".

Understandably the Tao is not a cultural God because it is not worshipped but the Tao is the source of everything including the Gods. However, in distinguishing between the DIVINE and the cultural Gods I regard the Tao as the DIVINE because as you read the rest of the chapter you would learn that it has all the characteristics of the DIVINE. For instance it existed before heaven and earth, it has no form, it operated everywhere, it is the mother of the universe and it is nameless.

The cultural Gods on the other hand came from us, they have different images, and they are culture bound. We erroneously claim that they created the universe, but unlike the DIVINE they have names. It is very important to get this difference clear in our minds. The one unites us while the other separates us. What separates us cannot be good for us. What unites us is there for everyone and there are no requirements. Here is chapter 1 of the Tao Te Ching:

The Tao that can be told is not the eternal Tao;
The name that can be named is not the eternal name.
The Nameless is the origin of Heaven and Earth;
The Named is the mother of all things.
There was something undifferentiated and yet complete,
Which existed before Heaven and Earth.
Soundless and formless it depends on nothing and does not change.
It operates everywhere and is free from danger.
It may be considered the mother of the universe.
I do not know its name; I call it Tao.
All things in the world come from being.
And being comes from non-being. (form comes from formlessness)?

My favorite Tao Te Ching Teaching is Wu Wei. Wu Wei is a doctrine in which we are able to do more with little effort by surrendering to the Tao. In his book, "The Seven Spiritual Laws of Success", Deepak Chopra referred to it as the Law of Least Effort. According to Lao Tze, author of the Tao Te Ching, "An integral being knows without going, sees without looking, and accomplishes without doing".

In his Book Ageless Body, Timeless Mind, Deepak Chopra

explains the Law of Least Effort as follows: *"The people who succeed best at any endeavor are generally following a pattern of handling their desires without undue struggle with their environment.-they are in the flow. ---they allow the solution (to their problem) to present itself, trusting their own abilities to cope with difficult challenges. By creating a minimum of anxiety, conflict, worry and false expectation, they promote highly efficient use of their mental and physical energies" p.104.*

How often have you struggled with your environment? How often have you tried too hard to get what you want? Are you trying too hard to impress your future partner to propose? Are you submitting too many applications for work without any results? Are you spending too much time thinking of due dates and accomplishing little? Are you trying many things to improve your health without success? Are you thinking too much about the future and neglecting the present? Relax and know the Tao. Let go and let the Tao take over! Let the doctrine of Wu Wei or the Law of Least Effort guide you toward a balanced and fulfilled life!

Thank you for reading this far. My intention is to expose you to the famous sacred texts of the world. You can see from the narrative that sacred texts are all over the world. As I said earlier they are not the direct words of the DIVINE but cultural experiences of the people. In this sense none of them is superior to the other apart from individual preferences or familiarity. Admittedly some sacred texts may contain passages that are at variance with our present understanding, but that is why we have minds to critically examine everything that is presented to us. However nothing is wrong from learning from the sacred texts but it is not necessary to believe in them. The problem with believing in a written work is the fact that the world is not static. What is true today may be questionable tomorrow. Besides foreign sacred texts are not the works of your people and should always be in a subordinate position. I am aware that some of you were born with foreign sacred texts and you have grown to regard them as your own. If you have read this book up to this point you may have the feeling that you have believed in something that has nothing to do with your life. Moving forward from here may seem difficult but believe me you can do it. It is better to be with the WHOLE than with any of the parts. Choose the DIVINE according to your experiences and the experiences of your people and I know that you'll be glad you did! Bear this in mind as you meditate on this book: all we want is to share our own experiences with our descendants and the world instead of other people's experiences. Let us make the DIVINE shine with our historical experiences. Write the African Testament of GOD!

NEW WORLD SPIRITUAL VISION

A New World is rising — not of nations or religions, but of Spirit.
The age of fear is ending. The reign of separation is falling.
Humanity awakens to its divine inheritance,
to the eternal truth that **God is not above us — God is within us.**

This is the Vision of the New World:
A civilization reborn in unity, guided by love,
anchored in the wisdom of the ancestors,
and illuminated by the living presence of the Divine in all creation.

The Divine is One, Infinite, and Immanent:
The Divine is not confined to heavens or temples.
The Divine breathes through all that lives.
Every being, every atom, every star is a reflection of the One Life.
We shall no longer seek God in distant skies,
but in the sacred pulse of existence — within and around us.

Humanity is the Living Image of the Divine
Each soul is a spark of the Infinite Fire.
To know oneself is to know the Divine.
No person is born unholy; no life is without purpose.
The journey of spirituality is the remembrance
of our eternal divine identity and creative power.

The Family is the First Sacred Temple
Before temples of stone were raised,
the family was the altar of divine communion.
In the love of mother and father, in the laughter of children,
the Divine builds its dwelling place on earth.

A family that honors truth and harmony
becomes a pillar of the New World Order of Spirit.

The Earth is the Living Body of the Divine

The Earth is not a possession but a sacred being.
The mountains are her bones, the rivers her blood,
the forests her breath, and humanity her consciousness.
To wound the Earth is to desecrate the Divine.
We pledge to walk gently, to restore balance,
and to live as guardians — not masters — of creation.

The Ancestors are the Living Memory of God

Those who walked before us are not dead;
they are transformed, guiding us from unseen realms.
Their wisdom flows through our veins,
their voices whisper in our dreams.
We honor the ancestors not through fear,
but through continuation — fulfilling their sacred dreams in our
time.

Truth is One, Though Paths are Many

No single book can contain the Infinite.
No single prophet can monopolize the Divine.
All sacred paths, when rooted in love and truth,
lead to the same Eternal Source.
We celebrate diversity, not as division,
but as the Divine expressing itself in countless forms.

Love is the Supreme Law of the Universe

Beyond creed, beyond doctrine, beyond race — Love is the law.
Love is the rhythm of creation,
the healer of wounds, the bridge between souls.
In every act of compassion, the Divine becomes visible.
Let Love be our doctrine, our politics, our economy, our prayer.

Revelation is Born Within
The age of blind obedience has ended.
The Spirit speaks directly to every awakened heart.
The truest scripture is the one written in the soul.
We listen inwardly, guided not by fear, but by inner light.
Each person becomes a prophet when they live in truth.

Humanity is One Sacred Family
No race is superior, no people are forgotten.
The divisions of history dissolve in the fire of awakening.
From Africa to Asia, from the Americas to Europe,
the Divine breath beats in one rhythm.
We are not strangers — we are reflections of the same Source.

The Future Belongs to Spiritual Civilization
The New World shall not be built by weapons or wealth,
but by awakened hearts and illumined minds.
Justice, peace, and wisdom shall replace dogma and domination.
The temples of tomorrow will be built from compassion,
and the scripture of the future will be written in deeds of love.

The Call of the New World
We stand at the threshold of a new dawn.
Let the religions of fear yield to the faith of freedom.
Let humanity rise as one sacred body —
each soul a flame of divine awareness,
each life a verse in the unfolding Testament of God.

The New World Spiritual Vision is not a religion —
It is the awakening of the Divine Human.
It is the remembrance that **we are the voice, the vessel, and the vision of God.**

Foundation of Marriage

The foundation of a strong marriage is built on commitment, trust, and respect, supported by open communication, shared values, and emotional connection. Other key elements include honesty, teamwork, and a willingness to resolve conflict. A strong foundation requires a couple to be a team with aligned goals and expectations, and to consistently nurture their bond through dedicated time and effort. Here are some thoughts on the foundation of marriage:

*Decide to be married to your partner for the rest of your life.
* Move in with the DIVINE.
* Leave your individual friends at the temple gate.
* Let Equality guide your home.
* Live with your spouse not a dream.
* Esteem your marriage above all.
* Enjoy a daily spiritual communion.
* Have a shared vision.
* Have a mission statement
* Love each other unconditionally.
* Hold onto Truth in all your interactions.
* Share all your resources equally.
* Disclose all individual financial activities.
* Take family classes and seminars yearly.
* Look at understanding before you react.
* Make up immediately after a disagreement.
* Resolve your problems without external help.
* Renew your vows after every 7 years.
* Do not highlight your individual contributions.
* Accept each other as you are and grow together.
* Know your spouse well.
* Appreciate each other.
* Enjoy an open communication.
* Do not criticize each other.
* Do not complain unnecessarily.
* Forgive each other completely.
* Apologize when you hurt your spouse.

* Trust each other completely.
* Be faithful to each other completely.
* Contribute proportionally in all you do.
* Enjoy a vacation once every year.
* Be sensitive to your partner's need for intimacy.
* Change yourself, not your partner.
* Rest your strength on the DIVINE, not your partner.
* Seek professional help when needed.

Responsible Family

A responsible family is built on mutual support, open communication, and a shared commitment to creating a safe and happy environment. Key aspects include each member being accountable for their actions, contributing to household duties, and adults providing for the family's financial, emotional, and physical needs. Teaching children responsibility is crucial for their development, encouraging them to be accountable for their choices and contribute to family life. Here are some thoughts on the Responsible Family:

* The DIVINE is at the head of the Responsible Family.
* Love each other unconditionally.
* Have daily prayers and meditations.
* Have daily family disclosure meetings.
* Live together with a shared vision.
* Have a family Mission Statement.
* Lean on your family Values.
* Be truthful in your interactions.
* Disclose all your activities.
* Be proactive in your relationships.
* Make up immediately after a disagreement.
* Esteem your family above all.
* Be loyal to your family.
* Be patient with your family.
* Refrain from complaining about each member.
* Do not compete with each other.

* Do not compare your family to others.
* Be an ambassador to your family.
* Know your family well with one-on-one visits.
* Listen attentively to your family.
* Appreciate each other's contributions.
* Enjoy an open communication.
* Do not criticize each other.
* Forgive when you are hurt.
* Apologize when you hurt anyone.
* Do not abuse your family.
* Trust each other completely.
* Take family growth classes and seminars every year.
* Have a family vacation once every year.
* Enjoy a weekly entertainment and games.
* Exercise regularly.
* Help the children with homework and assignments.
* Support the children's school play and games.
* Be sensitive to each person's need for a hug.
* Resolve your problems without external intervention.
* Seek professional help when needed.

Universal Spiritual Family Values
Universal spiritual family values include core tenets like love, compassion, forgiveness, respect, and responsibility. These values form the foundation for a family's spiritual life, promoting a sense of unity, mutual support, and a connection to something greater than themselves. Key practices include fostering a spirit of care and celebration for one another, encouraging personal growth, and sharing a common belief system or ethical framework. The following Universal Spiritual Family Values are attributed to the Sonari Family:

At the head of our family is the DIVINE.
Let the DIVINE within each of you be present in your family and avoid worshipping cultural Gods or depending on saviors.

We respect our parents and we love our children.
Parents love your children without conditions. Children love and

respect your parents.

Our family mission statement is our compass
Write your family mission statement today. A family without a mission statement could end up any where!

We give in abundance with joy, love and humility
Do not hesitate to give to whoever asks because that meeting is a spiritual moment.

Our educational goals have no limits
Engage in lifelong learning and you will experience joy and happiness all the days of your life.

We share our talents through work, art and science.
Have a hobby, an occupation or a career. It will enrich your life.

Our daily devotion strengthens our connection with the sacred
Make it a duty to pray and meditate daily.

We enjoy the fruits of communication and cooperation.
Have a daily disclosure meeting and share your life with your family.

Our commitment to wellness improves the quality of our lives.
Eat mostly seeds, fruits, nuts and vegetables. Exercise regularly and meditate daily.

We spend wisely and save for the "rainy days" of life
"Spend a little and save a lot" because there is no guarantee that you'll have your means of livelihood for the rest of your life.

Our family time enriches our relationships
Play games, take vacations and do things together like crabbing, fishing, hiking, studying, cleaning, cooking and so on.

We support marital activities only in marriage
Use your time to plan your life. You will be happy that you did

later. Most of our problems arise from making choices when we are not ready. Save yourself from unnecessary heartache, disease and unplanned pregnancy.

Universal Love

Universal love is a boundless, selfless, and unconditional form of love and acceptance for all beings, flowing in all directions without expectation of return. It is based on the wisdom of interconnectedness, extending beyond personal relationships to embrace everyone and everything in the universe. This love promotes feelings of friendliness, gentleness, and compassion, and is considered a foundation for a more peaceful and harmonious world. Here are some thoughts on LOVE:

LOVE is the underlying MYSTERY of the Universe.
LOVE has no Sacred Texts but pervades the Universe.
LOVE has no chosen people but is within all creatures.
LOVE enriches the life of every creature in the Universe.
LOVE nourishes all creatures without conditions or requirements.
You are loved irrespective of the choices you make or have made in the past.
You are loved without regard to your race, color, nationality, culture or belief.
LOVE is not concerned with your birth circumstances or social status.
LOVE does not care about your affiliation or position in life.
LOVE only cares for your good and well being.
You are a hereditary heir and custodian of LOVE.
And anyone who realizes this TRUTH is not only saved
But will also be healed, be prosperous, be joyful and be at peace.

Universal Love Prayers

A Universal Love Prayer seeks to transcend religious doctrines, addressing a higher power or universal consciousness to foster compassion, forgiveness, and unity among all people and beings. It draws on common themes from various faith traditions, and from the circular world. Here are some notable Universal Love prayers for your family:

Universal Love Payer by Dr. Sonari
O GOD who pervades the Universe,
we thank You for Your loving Presence.
You have blessed all things
and entrusted us with the secret of creation.

Your presence is our guiding light,
and Your love our ornament and strength.
Protect us from evil
and heal us of all infirmities.

Lead us at the crossroads of life,
reassure us when doubts arise,
be our guide when we feel helpless,
and impress upon our hearts that You are near.

Grant us courage to ignite the light within us,
and let it glow wherever we go,
that we may help others see their own lights—
for our own enlightenment and for the triumph of Universal Love.

Universal Love Prayer by Google AI
O Divine Source of all that is,
We turn to you with open hearts, seeking the perfection of love, harmony, and beauty. Guide us to recognize the sacred spark of your presence in every being we meet, and to treat one another

with kindness, compassion, and respect.

Illuminate our minds with clarity, that we may understand our shared humanity despite our diverse paths. Soften our hearts with empathy, so we may feel the pain of others and be moved to ease their suffering.

Grant us the courage to forgive, for ourselves and for others, releasing the burdens of the past. Help us build bridges where there are divides and sow peace where there is conflict. May our words be vessels of healing and hope, and our actions be driven by selfless love.

We pray for all beings on this earth: For those who are suffering, that they may find comfort. For those who are lonely, that they may find companionship. For those who are filled with fear, that they may find courage. For those who are full of anger, that their hearts may be softened.

May all beings be well.
May all beings be peaceful.
May all beings be free from suffering.

Let our lives be a testament to your infinite love. Unite us as one family, and may we walk together on this sacred earth with mutual respect and understanding, working toward the good of all.

Universal Love Prayer by GEMINI AI

May our hearts be open to receive and give unconditional love, recognizing the DIVINE spark within all beings.

May we see beyond difference and division, acknowledging our fundamental interconnection—that the well-being of one is tied to the well-being of all.

For those who suffer, may comfort and healing find them. For those who are lost, may a path to peace and clarity be revealed to them. For those who are oppressed, may justice and freedom prevail now.

Grant us the courage to forgive, the wisdom to understand, and the humility to learn from one another. May we be instruments of peace, speaking words that heal and performing actions that uplift.

Let love be our guide in every thought, word, and deed, binding the tapestry of humanity together with kindness, compassion, and respect.

May all beings everywhere be happy, free, and safe.

Universal Love Prayer by COPILOT AI
Divine Source of all life, From every corner of the Earth, we gather in spirit— Beyond borders, beyond names, beyond beliefs— To honor the sacred bond that connects us all.

May love rise like the sun in every heart, Warming the cold, healing the broken, Guiding the lost, and uplifting the weary.

Let kindness be our language, And empathy our compass. May we see the DIVINE in every face, And hear truth in every voice.

Where there is hatred, sow peace. Where there is fear, plant courage. Where there is division, build bridges.

We ask not for perfection, But for the grace to grow, To forgive, to listen, and to love without condition.

May this prayer ripple outward— Touching every soul, every creature, every leaf— Until the whole world sings in harmony.

Universal Love Prayer by ChatGPT
Divine Source of All That Is,

From the heart of creation, we call upon Your boundless love.
Let Your light awaken every soul to the truth —
that we are One breath, One life, One family.

May love rise where fear once lived.
May understanding bridge the walls of differences.
May compassion be the law written upon every heart.

Bless the earth and all her children —
human, animal, plant, and spirit —
that harmony may return to our shared home.

Teach us to forgive as freely as the wind blows,
to give as abundantly as the sun shines,
and to serve with hands guided by peace.

Let our thoughts be seeds of kindness,
our words rivers of healing,
and our actions instruments of DIVINE unity.

Today, we choose love —
not as a feeling alone,
but as the sacred power that restores the world.

May all beings be free.
May all hearts be whole.
May all creation live in love.

Universal Love Prayer by Claude. AI
May love awaken in every heart, boundless as the sky, gentle as morning light.

May we see beyond the walls we build, recognizing in each face a mirror of our own longing, our own hope, our own sacred worth.

May compassion flow like rivers meeting the sea, dissolving the illusion of separation, reminding us we are waves in one vast ocean.

May we offer kindness without condition, forgiveness without keeping score, and presence without distraction.

May the suffering know comfort, the lonely know belonging, the lost know direction, and the broken know healing.

May we love not only those who love us back, but extend our care to the stranger, the different, the difficult, knowing that love grows strongest when given freely, without return.

May we tend the earth with reverence, honor all living things as kin, and protect what is precious and fragile.

May we be brave enough to love in a world that sometimes forgets how, holding space for joy and sorrow alike, knowing both are threads in the fabric of connection.

And may we remember: love is not something we find, but something we become, something we practice, something we are.

May it be so.

Universal Love Prayer by DeepAI
Divine Source of All That Is,
We come before You with open hearts and humble spirits.
May Your infinite love flow through us, illuminating every corner of our being.

Help us to see beyond differences, to embrace all beings with compassion and kindness.
May love be our guiding light in thoughts, words, and actions.

Grant us the grace to forgive, to understand, and to accept.

May we recognize the DIVINE presence in ourselves and in everyone we encounter.

May love unite us beyond borders, beliefs, and boundaries, Fostering peace, harmony, and unity on this beautiful Earth.

Thank You for the gift of love, the greatest power of all. May we share it freely and generously, now and always.

Universal Love Prayer by DeepSeek AI

Source of All Love,
Open my heart to love myself fully.
Guide my actions to love others deeply.
Inspire my spirit to love this world completely.
May I be a clear channel for kindness, compassion, and connection today and always
And so it is.

Universal Love Prayer by AIChatting

In the stillness of this moment,
I open my heart to the essence of love.
May love flow through me and illuminate my being,
Connecting me to all creatures,
Across time and space.

I embrace the diversity of humanity,
Honoring each soul's journey and truth.
May understanding and compassion blossom,
As I seek to see the world through the eyes of others,
Recognizing our shared hopes and dreams.

With every breath, I send love to those who suffer,
To the lonely, the lost, and the grieving.

May they find comfort, healing, and peace,
And may my actions reflect kindness,
To uplift and support all in need.

Let love be the guiding light in my life,
In thoughts, words, and deeds.
May I cultivate patience and forgiveness,
Releasing judgment and embracing acceptance,
As we walk this path together.

I send love to the Earth and all her inhabitants,
Seeking harmony with nature and respect for all life.
May our shared home thrive in balance and beauty,
Nurtured by our collective care and responsibility.

As a vessel of love, I radiate goodwill,

Universal Spiritual Values

Universal spiritual values are core principles shared across cultures and faiths, such as love, compassion, honesty, integrity, gratitude, humility, forgiveness, tolerance, patience, justice, peace, courage, wisdom, hope, service, self-control, harmony, respect for others, accountability, and interconnectedness, which guide ethical behavior and personal growth. These values are often cultivated through practices like prayer and meditation and can be categorized into different areas, including altruistic, humanistic, and personal values. Here are some thoughts on Universal Spiritual Values:

Love YOURSELF the way you are.
Your earthly journey is very complicated but loving YOURSELF makes it easy. How can you love yourself? You can love YOURSELF by maintaining a regular time for waking up and going to bed; eating healthy foods; keeping positive thoughts; being creative; having a source of employment; playing with your

family and friends; rewarding yourself regularly; exercising regularly; meditating regularly; wearing your favorite clothes once a week if you always dress up to work; dressing up once a week if you wear casual clothes to work; reading a book every month; living in the moment and taking yearly continuing education classes.

Love all creatures without conditions

LIFE loves you without conditions. How? You have everything you need for the journey: unconditional love irrespective of who you are; spiritual support to accomplish your dreams; fruits, seeds, nuts, roots and vegetables to nourish your body; water to quench your thirst; air to keep you alive; other creatures to keep you company and teachers to show you the way. Where else can you find such love? This indeed is the Greatest Love of all! In return you have a moral duty to love all creatures without conditions.

Give with Love, Humility and Joy

Make giving your way for life and it will change the ways of your life. You can give in many ways but before you give first be aware of your environment. Who needs help? Who can use a smile? Who needs to be motivated? Who needs an advice? Who needs to be encouraged? Who can use a little hope? Who is in need of some cash? Go about your day forgetting yourself and helping as many people as you can because sometimes it is when we help others that we find ourselves!

Improve yourself with constant Learning

If you are not learning you are stuck in life. Alternatively if you are not learning you are dying slowly. I know we are all dying but the death from not learning is worst than any natural death in the sense that you just wasted a lifetime! By all means learn and grow! You can learn by reading autobiographies of your favorite people, taking human development classes, attending seminars, reading sacred texts, taking college classes, taking self improvement classes and taking career development classes.

Develop yourself with daily meditation

If you want to know yourself practice regular meditation. Have time daily to sit and review your day. Meditation is also a time to pip into the future and create what you want the future to be. For instance your can create a normal day or a great day buy simply seeing what you want to happen in your mind's eye. If you want to create a great day you can begin to see yourself waking up refreshed and happy in the morning; going to work and observing the people, animals, birds, plants and flowers on your way; greeting members of your work place as you go to your office or work area; doing your work with confidence and efficiently; and overcoming all challenges with ease. Try it and you may be surprised how things worked out for you on that day.

Eat mostly nuts, fruits, seeds and vegetables
Because of the nature of our modern society many people do not eat right anymore and the choices we make on food in our younger years show up as health problems in our later years.
If we are thinking right we could all realize that if the body dies it must be delicate and should be handled with care. We should all take time to choose our drinks and the food we eat and the best choice we can make is to eat natural foods and avoid man-made foods and drinks. I know it is not easy but with practice eating natural food could become second nature.

Energize your body with regular exercise
Doing a regular form of exercise is very important for your well being. For instance exercise controls weight, it helps you to sleep better, it improves your mood, it helps to prevent some diseases and it energizes your body. There are many ways to exercise and in some cases you don't even need to spend money to exercise. If you want to spend money enrolling in a gym and going to the gym regularly is a good way to exercise. If you do not want to spend money you can just walk about a couple of miles every day or you could also exercise in your living room by stretching, doing jumping jack, lifting weights, or doing some form of floor exercise.

Manage your life with a mission statement

Do you have a mission statement? I mean do you have a destination in life apart from the natural destination for all of us? The destination could be what you want to become or what you want to do in life. For instance you may want to become a doctor, an attorney, a dentist or a sanitary engineer. On the other hand you may want to sing, dance, act, paint, draw, program or something like that. A mission statement helps you to have a handle on your life and the direction you want it to go. You may temporarily deviate from your goal because of circumstances but the mission statement helps you to get up and continue the journey toward your destination.

Live in the moment with love, peace and happiness

This moment is all you have so it is wise to make it worthwhile. How can you live in the moment? You can visit your parents and share your love. You can reconnect with an old friend. You can go fishing or hiking. You can also write a book. In short you can do many things today that could make you happy and possibly influence your tomorrows. However do not worry about tomorrow and do not regret about yesterday because you've got today.

Share the message of Universal Love

The message of Universal Love states that "You are loved without conditions and you are blessed without requirements". This is a very difficult truth to grasp because we have all been indoctrinated to believe that we are sinners and that we need to do something in order to be forgiven. This is not true because LIFE treats all of us the same way irrespective of religion, race, color or nationality. Consider the snow..... does it stop you from playing in it because of what you did or the color of your skin? No it doesn't. In the same way LIFE does not discriminate against you. LIFE just wants you to be fulfilled. So when next you meet a friend, family member or a total stranger just say "You are loved without conditions and you are blessed without requirements.

Jewels of Life

The term "Jewels of life" refers to a list of virtues or principles that guide a person toward a meaningful existence. While the exact wording can vary, the most common list includes knowledge, wisdom, understanding, freedom, justice, equality, food, clothing, shelter, love, peace, and happiness. These are often presented in a specific order, starting with intellectual and moral virtues and progressing to physical and emotional needs, ultimately leading to happiness through love and peace. Here are some thoughts that reflect the Jewels of Life:

* Think of the DIVINE within you always.
* Love all creatures unconditionally.
* Get a good education.
* Do not kill any creature.
* Use thought to create and to heal.
* Do not take what does not belong to you.
* Have marital activities ONLY in marriage.
* Exercise regularly and drink enough water.
* Keep the Earth clean and avoid polluting it.
* Mostly eat nuts, seeds, fruits, and vegetables.
* Refrain from uttering cursing and hateful words.
* Act with Truth, and Love, in all your transactions.
* Use languages to convey love, truth, and kindness.
* Respect all beliefs and avoid forcing your beliefs on others.
* Have a Mission on Earth statement to guide you on your journey.
* Avoid all degrading materials including pornography and violence.
* Be responsive to the civic duties of your town, state, country and planet.
* Do not drink, smoke or eat anything that could alter the peace within your body.
* Avoid owning or using guns, firearms, chemical, biological and

nuclear weapons.

* Pray and meditate when you wake up in the morning and when you retire at night.

* Give what you can to whoever asks and support the physically or mentally challenged.

* Have a career, a vocation, a trade or an occupation that contributes to the general good.

* Respect all creatures and demonstrate understanding for all differences in the Universe.

* Share the message of Universal Love with all creatures to inspire, educate, motivate and to heal.

* Make each moment you live a moment of love, peace and happiness for yourself and for everyone you meet.

Bibliography

Achebe, Chinua. Things Fall Apart. Anchor Books, New York, NY USA 1994

Allen, James. As I Think. DeVorss & Company Publisher, Marina del Ray, CA 1991

Armstrong, Karen. A History of God: The 4,000-Year Quest of Judaism, Christianity and Islam. Ballantine Books. 1993

Beck, Renee & Metrick, Sydney Barbara. The Art of Ritual: Creating & Performing ceremonies for Growth & Change. Celestial Arts. Berkeley, CA USA 2003

Biziou, Barbara. The Joy of Rituals. Golden Books. New York, NY USA 1999

Campbell, Joseph. The Power of Myth. Anchor Books. New York, NY USA 1991

Campbell, Joseph. Creative Mythology: The Masks of God. Penguin Books. 1976

Campbell, Joseph. Myths to Live By. Bantam Books. 1988

Campbell, Joseph. Occidental Mythology: The Masks of God. Penguin Books. 1976

Campbell, Joseph. Oriental Mythology: The Masks of God. Penguin Books. 1976

Campbell, Joseph. Primitive Mythology: The Masks of God. Penguin Books. 1976

Campbell, Joseph. Transformation of Myth Through Time. Harper & Row. 1990

Capra, Fritjof. The Tao of Physics. Shambala, Boston, MA, USA 1991

Carus, Paul. The Gospel of Buddha. The Open Court Publishing Company. 1995.

Correal, Tobe Melora. Finding Soul on the Path of Orisha. Crossing Press, Berkely, USA, 2003

Dawkins, Richard. The GOD Delusion. Black Swan. 2006

Eck, Diana L. A New Religious America: How a "Christian Country" has become the World's Most Religiously Diverse Nation. HarperSanFrancisco, New York, NY, USA 2001

Eckel, Malcolm David. Great World Religions: Buddhism. The Teaching Company, Chantilly, Virginia, USA 2003

Eliopoulos, Charlotte. Invitation to Holistic Health: A Guide to Living a Balanced Life. Jones & Bartlett Publishers, Sudbury, MA USA 2004

Esposito, John L. Great World Religions: Islam. The Teaching Company, Chantilly, Virginia, USA 2003

Ford, Clyde W. The Hero with an African Face: Mythic Wisdom of Traditional Africa Bantam Books. 2000.

Gafni, Isaiah M. Great World Religions: Judaism. The Teaching Company, Chantilly, Virginia, USA 2003

Gonzalez-Wippler, Migene. Santeria, the Religion. Llewellyn Publications, St Paul, Mincsotc, USA, 1994.

Griffith, Tom. Confucius, The Analects. Wordsworth Classics, Cumberland House,
Hertfordshire, England 1996.

Haught, James A. Holy Horrors: An Illustrated History of Religious Murder and Madness.

Hitchcock, Mark: 2012 The Bible and the end of the world.
Harvest House Publishers, Eugene, Oregon
Prometheus Books, Amherst, NY USA 1990

Huntley, Karyl. Real Life Rituals. Spiritual Living Press, Burbank, CA 2005

Johnson, Luke Timothy. Great World Religions: Christianity. The Teaching Company, Chantilly, Virginia, USA 2003

Jones, Charles B. Introduction to the Study of Religion. The Teaching Company, Chantilly, Virginia, USA 2008

Karade, Baba Ifa. The Handbook of Yoruba Religious Concepts. Weiser Books, Boston MA, USA 1994

Kimball, Charles. Comparative Religion. The Teaching Company,

Chantilly, Virginia, USA 2008

Kyle, Richard. A History of the End Times. Baker Books, Grand Rapids, Michigan.

Lau, D. C. Lao Tzu Tao Te Ching. Penguin Books. Harmondsworth, Middlesex, England, 1963

Laye, Camara. The African Child. Nelson House, Surrey, UK 1980

Mascaro, Juan. The Bhagavad Gita. Penguin Classics, Harmondsworth, Middlesex, England, 1987

Mascaro, Juan. The Dhammapada. Penguin Classics, London, England, 1973

Mascaro, Juan. The Upanishads. Penguin Books, London, England, 1965

Miller, Barbara Stoler. The Bhagavad-Gita. Bantam Books, Newyork, NewYork.

Muesse, Mark William. Great World Religions: Hinduism. The Teaching Company, Chantilly, Virginia, USA 2003

Muesse, Mark W. Religions of the Axial Age: An Approach to the World's Religions. The Teaching Company, Chantilly, Virginia, USA 2007

Muesse, Mark W. Great World Religions: Hinduism. The Teaching Company, Chantilly, Virginia, USA 2003

Olivelle, Patrick. Upanishads. Oxford University Press.

Perceival, Harold W. Thinking & Destiny. The Word Foundation, Dallas, TX USA 1974

Prabhavananda, Swami & Manchester, Frederick. The Upanishads, Breath of the Eternal. A Mentor Book. New York, New York, USA 1948

Prothero, Stephen. God is not One: The Eight Rival Religions that run the World. HarperOne, New York, NY USA 2010

Redfield, James. The Celestial Vision: Living the New Spiritual Awareness. Warner Books. 1997.

Schmidt, Roger. Exploring Religion. Wadsworth Publishing Company. 1988

Smith, Wilfred Cantwell. Patterns of Faith around the World. One

World Publications, Oxford, England. 1998
Thomas, Hugh. The Slave Trade: The Story of the Atlantic Slave
Trade: 1440-1870. Simon & Schuster, New York, NY 1997
Thompson, Norma H. Religious Pluralism & Religious
Education.Religious Education Press, Birmingham, AL, USA 1988
Uhl, Stephen Frederick. Out of God's Closet. Golden Rule
Publishers. 2009
Vidyalankar, Pandit Satyakam. The Holy Vedas: A Golden
Treasury. Clarion Books.
Wilson, Andrew. World Scripture: A Comparative Anthology of
Sacred Texts. Paragon House, New York, NY 1991

Other Sources

Holy Bible: New international Version.Zondervan Bible
Publishers. 1978
Rig Veda: Sacred Writings. Hinduism. Translated by Ralph T. H.
Griffith
The Book of Mormon: Another Testament of Jesus Christ. The
Church of Jesus Christ of Latter Day Saints. 1981
The Quran: The Final Testament. Translated by Rashad Khalifa,
Ph.D. Universal Unity, Fremont, CA 1992
The Tanakh. The Jewish Publication Society. 1985
The Universal Holy Book: A spiritual Text for All Faiths and
Beliefs. Soteme Publishing, Portland, OR USA. 2009

AI
Deep.Ai, Gemini, Copilot, CHATGPT, DeepSeek, Claude.Ai,
Quillbot, HotBot, Julius, AiChatting.

Copilot References

- Mbiti, John S. *African Religions and Philosophy*. Heinemann, 1969.
- Gyekye, Kwame. *African Cultural Values: An Introduction*. Sankofa Publishing, 1996.
- Wiredu, Kwasi. *Philosophy and an African Culture*. Cambridge University Press, 1980.
- Asante, Molefi Kete. *Afrocentricity: The Theory of Social Change*. African American Images, 2003.
- Abiodun, Rowland. *Yoruba Art and Language: Seeking the African in African Art*. Cambridge University Press, 2014.

Julius References
References

Armstrong, Karen. *A History of God: The 4,000-Year Quest of Judaism, Christianity, and Islam*. Ballantine Books, 1993.

Esposito, John L. *Islam: The Straight Path*. Oxford University Press, 2016.

Heschel, Abraham Joshua. *God in Search of Man: A Philosophy of Judaism*. Farrar, Straus and Giroux, 1955.

McGrath, Alister E. *Christian Theology: An Introduction*. Wiley-Blackwell, 2016.

Smith, Huston. *The World's Religions*. HarperOne, 1991.

DeepSeek References
References & Further Reading:

- Mbiti, John S. *African Religions and Philosophy*.
- Idowu, E. Bolaji. *Olodumare: God in Yoruba Belief*.
- Tempels, Placide. *Bantu Philosophy*.

- Gyekye, Kwame. *An Essay on African Philosophical Thought: The Akan Conceptual Scheme.*
- Some, Malidoma Patrice. *Of Water and the Spirit: Ritual, Magic, and Initiation in the Life of an African Shaman.*
- Zahan, Dominique. *The Religion, Spirituality, and Thought of Traditional Africa.*

www.ingramcontent.com/pod-product-compliance
Lightning Source LLC
Chambersburg PA
CBHW072155090426
42740CB00012B/2271